Homeowner's Guide to Fireplaces

R. J. Lytle and Marie-Jeanne Lytle

Ideals Publishing Corp.

Milwaukee, Wisconsin

Table of Contents

ISBN 0-8249-6105-6

Copyright © 1981 by Ideals Publishing Corporation

Published by Ideals Publishing Corporation
11315 Watertown Plank Road
Milwaukee, Wisconsin 53226

Editor, David Schansberg

Cover photo courtesy of Martin Industries

⌂ SUCCESSFUL
HOME IMPROVEMENT SERIES

Bathroom Planning and Remodeling
Kitchen Planning and Remodeling
Space Saving Shelves and Built-ins
Finishing Off Additional Rooms
Finding and Fixing the Older Home
Money Saving Home Repair Guide
Homeowner's Guide to Tools
Homeowner's Guide to Electrical Wiring
Homeowner's Guide to Plumbing
Homeowner's Guide to Roofing and Siding
Homeowner's Guide to Fireplaces
Home Plans for the '80s
How to Build Your Own Home

Introduction

A home without a fireplace does seem to lack something—a certain something that is the heart of the home. It is true that we no longer need a fireplace in each room in order to survive the cold of the winter. There is an element of security, however, in knowing that you could have a fire if necessary. The pioneer spirit still lives within us.

Although fireplaces are no longer necessary for survival, a working fireplace with a cheerful fire blazing away exudes an atmosphere of happy congenial living and contributes to the feeling that this is the good life! Even during the hot summer months, the mind envisions the image of a crackling fire and enjoys the atmosphere of hospitality, rest and repose that is in the mind's eye. A fireplace suggests the comfort and contentment of quiet evenings before a blazing hearth.

Before we go on more deeply into the planning and building of a fireplace, let us first of all remember this good rule: "Never lose sight of the fact that the most important factor for a fireplace is the fire itself." In following this rule, the designer of the fireplace must stay with a relatively simple fireplace, installed at moderate costs on well-tested principles, using locally available materials.

A common evil exists in the vast number of fireplaces intended to provide fireside satisfaction, but which fail to do so through faulty construction. This may result from ignorance or inattention at a time when the owner is occupied with other features of his home project. It may reflect somebody's mistaken effort to hold down costs, or merely the absence of suitable plans to crystallize intentions and to guide against errors.

It is almost as easy to build a successful fireplace as to build a bad one. Certain principles must be observed. Those principles are embodied in the drawings and directions to be found in ensuing chapters.

Besides these positive guides, common mistakes are pointed out and discussed in later chapters.

The fireplace you are entitled to have for your money invested is a fireplace in which fires kindle readily, burn smoothly, yield generous heat, and discharge smoke and gases *up* the flue.

It is the purpose of this book to help you in solving the problems that confront anyone looking forward to the ownership of a fireplace, whether in a home to be built or an interior to be remodeled.

This chapter begins by mentioning the different types of fireplaces, the important features of each to assist in a reasonable choice. Later chapters will explain in detail the necessary instructions for success with each type.

One of the major decisions that you will have to make with your family is "what type of fireplace?" If you have the space and can afford it, you will probably choose the ever-popular masonry fireplace. Desire for heat from the fireplace may lead to a heat-circulating fireplace. Concern about power blackouts, oil embargoes, or simply utility-company ineptitude, may compel you to think of the fireplace as an emergency or supplementary source of heat. Heat-circulating fireplaces, pre-builts, or wood-burning stoves can be the answer. A remodeling project may suggest a pre-built, gas, or electric fireplace.

A wide range of styles and types of masonry fireplaces have developed over the years. Beyond the traditional fireplace in the wall there are corner fireplaces in both exterior and interior corners, fireplaces in which the flame is visible in two or three directions, double opening fireplaces that serve two rooms on opposite sides of a partition wall, and hooded fireplaces.

A heat-circulating fireplace is another general type of fireplace which gives you more heat for your fuel than the masonry fireplace. A circulator, like a furnace, gives you the bonus of the circulated, convection-heated air. This type of fireplace is most useful in a vacation cottage which has no furnace, or in a home where warmth is needed between the seasons but turning on the heat is not quite justified.

Pre-Built Fireplaces Although masonry fireplaces are most often preferred, they are not always possible for everyone. The pre-built fireplace offers excellent solutions to various problems. A pre-built makes it possible to install a woodburning fireplace without concrete footings, without a masonry chimney, at lower cost, and in a room where structural considerations would otherwise rule out a fireplace. The pre-built is a great boon to apartment dwellers, vacation home builders, and to folks remodeling their home or adding on a room.

There are two basic types of pre-built fireplaces; the "built-in pre-built," which is a conventional-appearing fireplace usually built into a wall, and the metal fireplace, usually freestanding.

Balcony from sleeping area looks into living room with two-story fireplace. Note wood storage under hearth. Photo courtesy of Deck House

Two-way fireplace centers on conversation group in living room, but also separates the dining area in the rear. Photo courtesy of Deck House

Fireplace in basement recreation room, flanked by bookcases, gives focus of interest to windowless walls. Photo courtesy of Joseph W. Molitor

Bedroom fireplace makes for pleasant dreams and offers morning and evening warmth. Photo courtesy of Glen Allison

The built-in pre-built fireplace is usually built into a conventional setting with a brick or woodpaneled wall and with a slate, tile, or other hearth. It is difficult to identify as metal or pre-built. The metal fireplace, on the other hand, is obviously and attractively metal, with striking and unusual shapes available. Metal fireplaces come not only in a variety of shapes, but also in a rainbow of colors and materials. They can be made of black wrought iron, copper and many gorgeous colors of easy-to-clean porcelain on steel.

Stoves The ever-popular Franklin stove in America has long been the symbol of heating (and sometimes cooking) with wood. Since the oil embargo in the early 70s, interest in wood stoves has boomed. Today we have Scandinavian stoves, which were developed to meet a fuel shortage hundreds of years ago—a wood shortage. Copies of the old pot-bellied stove are now being manufactured with modern improvements. With some stoves it is possible to have the cheer of an open fire and, when needed, the efficient heating a well-designed stove provides.

Electric and Gas Fireplaces If it is not possible to have a wood- or coal-burning fireplace where you live, or you do not want to go through the mess of a solid fuel fire, and yet you crave the warmth and glow of a fire, do not despair—there is a solution! There are electric or gas fireplaces for low cost which give you the glow of the fire with no mess, and the added advantage of quick response—an instant cozy fire. The gas fireplace needs a vent but this is easily and economically installed.

Various Rooms It is a happy home that has a single living room fireplace, even if cost or architectural restrictions make it difficult to have this feature in any other room.

However, there are other locations for a fireplace besides the living room. One that comes readily to mind is a kitchen located in the rear of the living room. Here, employing the same chimney, a fireplace for cooking may logically be provided. It may be supplemented by gas or electric appliances in the same masonry installation.

The basement recreation room and the family room are places where many owners find joy in the presence

This new heat circulating fireplace provides heat exchange on all four sides of the firebox. Photo courtesy of Majestic

of a fireplace, either for warmth or casual cookery or both.

A library, study, or den—the personal room of studious individuals—gains charm from an open fire.

Bedroom fireplaces are less common than in days when open fires were the chief means of warming a house. Nevertheless, there are men and women today who like to dress and undress before an open fire—to lapse into slumber while a dying fire flickers its warmth.

Office and Club A physician whose waiting room contained a shielded and unused fireplace of a past era tells how he noted a better spirit in his patients after the fireplace was restored to use.

A club lounge or church reception room with an open fire promotes harmony of spirit.

There are many company offices in which a fireplace exerts a harmonizing influence in executive decisions or in conference deliberations.

In any of the situations discussed, the presence of a fireplace adds gracious dignity and prestige, as well as physical comfort and sociability.

Flush or Projecting A decision must be made between having the fireplace flush with the face of the

This fireplace insert also features heat exchange around the fire box. Photo courtesy of Fuego

Adobe fireplace in New Mexico home provides regional motif with a ceramic tile hearth. Photo courtesy of Glen Allison

wall or projected, wholly or partly, within the room. Several factors of planning are involved, including the treatment of the exterior of the chimney, in some cases. In others, it will be features of an adjacent room that determines the choice, perhaps kitchen cooking appliances that are vented into the same stack.

Reasons for projection into the room may be the desire to flank the fireplace with cabinets or shelving to hold books or ornaments. In the case of circulator fireplaces, there is the advantage of having hot air vents installed at the side of the projection, hence making them less conspicuous than when located in the face of the upper wall.

Satisfaction Through Simplicity We have discussed the various types of fireplaces and a few considerations governing the choice of the proper fireplace in order to give you a feel for the field as a whole. You'll be on surest ground, however, if your personal choice is for a relatively simple fireplace, installed at moderate costs on well-tested principles and using readily obtainable materials.

Above all, remember that the most important factor in any fireplace is the fire—flame has the same quality in a simple, low-cost fireplace as in the most elaborate structure.

Old-fashioned but efficient, this freestanding fireplace is an attractive and functional addition to this room. Photo courtesy of Ashley

Straight sleek lines of this black metal hood contrast against the rough masonry in the fieldstone fireplace wall. An interesting example of traditional materials in a modern interior. Photo courtesy of Hedrich-Blessing

Fireplace History

Man's command of fire is one of the oldest and most important factors in his slow rise to civilization. Various peoples have their myths about the origin of this important blessing. Greek mythology gives credit to the titan Prometheus. A titan was supposed to be a creature midway between a god and a man.

Prometheus, says the story, stole fire from Zeus, the great god of the Greeks, and brought it down to man, thus miraculously saving mankind from the destruction which Zeus had planned.

There is a symbolical meaning to the myth, since Prometheus, in the Greek tongue, means forethought—not a bad adjunct in any project involving fire.

In the realm of the fireplace, nothing is new and nothing old. The earliest known types of fireplaces are among the novelties of today. The latest innovations have a record of centuries behind them.

The earliest indoor use of fire seems, everywhere, to have meant a hearth in the central open space of a dwelling. Such hearths existed in Britain before the coming of the Romans. They are found today in the island habitations of the Hebrides and among the crofters of Scotland, with roof openings for the escape of smoke. Central hearths are not uncommon today among sophisticated seekers of novelty. A large one was erected in the center of a Chicago hotel lobby not long ago. However, these modern adaptations are fitted with inverted funnels to carry off the smoke—not mere holes in the roof.

When the Romans encountered early Britain's rainy and forbidding chill, they brought braziers, fire pans on legs, not unlike a certain present-day type of lawn barbecue. The Romans also practiced what some innovators now call radiant heating, by piping flame and smoke through passages in walls and floors.

The heat-circulating fireplace was invented in France about the year 1600, or a little later, and many times since. So instead of a sharply defined sequence of fireplace periods, we have a variety of forms that have existed in parallel over most of the eras of our study. The owner or designer of today's fireplace has great freedom in choosing forms, sizes and positions, but it is unlikely that he will create a wholly new type. On the other hand, no form that he can choose will be censured as outmoded.

The central hearth prevailed from earliest times until the sixteenth century, when the wall fireplace, first recorded in the tenth century, gained preference and became the prevailing type.

Central fires gave the occupants of the room all the benefit of direct radiation. The smoke eddying around the rafters and escaping through a roof opening must have deposited much soot and ash. But the offense may have been less than we imagine, for the fuel was wood, not the soot-breeding coal used in some fireplaces today. Yet Chaucer describes the apparel of the nun in his Canterbury Tales as being "full sooty."

Three incidental factors are worth mentioning. The hearth was often raised above the floor level, so there is nothing new about the "modern" elevation of the hearth. Smoke louvers, hollow, ventilated structures, surmounted the smoke opening and protected the interior against rain.

The third feature to be noted is that the andiron was not an ornamental device as it often is today. When cooking was part of the function of the central fire, it was necessary to have a support for the spits on which meat was suspended over the fire. Andirons, with prongs and notches, supported the ends of the spit. They also supported heavier crossbars on which pots were hung. To steady the two andirons, a crossbrace often joined them, being welded to each a few inches above hearth level. This cross member also supported sticks of firewood, slanted against it.

Two early chimney tops, when utility alone was not enough.

Early Persian design. Extreme enclosure would ensure smoke control but would limit heating value.

Dutch design—these were usually decorated with tiles, made at Delft.

Fireplaces Move to the Wall

When Norman barons commenced to build castles of more than one story, there was need for a means of heating upper and lower rooms separately, the central fire with roof outlet being no longer a possible resource. From this came the wall fireplace.

Fireplaces at the wall did not immediately mean chimneys, nor recesses in the wall. Most often, the fire was built on a hearth projecting forward from the masonry wall. Over the fire was a hood of metal or masonry, and back of the hood, at its upper extremity, was a hole extending slantwise through the wall that carried off the smoke.

Early hooded fireplaces generally lacked any side structure. Without jamb support, the hood was kept in place by a corbell or bracket anchored in the wall masonry. If the hood itself was of masonry construction, there was need of a lintel, which might be a heavy oak beam. Sometimes the side support also consisted of two wooden members, cantilevered through the thickness of the wall. Some old prints indicate hoods of semicircular section, but more often rectangular.

Partial recessing of the hearth followed, as well as the development of chimneys that carried the smoke above roof level. In the Gothic, or Tudor, period we find great elaboration of the chimney, as shown in the illustration on the previous page.

In the castles and mansions of aristocrats, it was feasible to have separate fireplaces in various rooms, primarily for warmth, while the kitchen fireplace was a separate development, primarily devoted to the preparation of food. A number of cooks, scullions and spit

Detail of tile design in similar fireplace. (Amsterdam Corp.)

Early Brittany, from a print. Note bed nook nearby.

Hooded corner fireplace, common to Sweden.

After Scandinavian style, in tile and sculptured plaster with pine paneling.

boys might find employment there.

In cottages and farmhouses, a single fireplace served both for warmth and for cookery. The later type usually had both a fire chamber and an enclosed oven, built into the masonry at one side. Occasionally there would be ovens on both sides. In any case there would be cranes, trivets, pots, pans, spits, etc.

Such fireplaces served colonial homes for generations, although prosperous folks might also have parlor fireplaces. Sometimes the kitchen type of fireplace would be very wide, so that the fire, occupying the central portion, left room for stools or benches in the "inglenook." Generally it was the privilege of the elderly to sit in the chimney corner.

Such fireplaces continued in practical service for many years and may, in out of the way places, be in use today.

The pioneer cooking fireplace, in a somewhat contracted and refined form, is the most frequently copied of any of the distinctly earlier types. And this is not mere antiquarian affectation. All over America we find casual meals being cooked much as our ancestors prepared them.

In Germany there was an early trend toward enclosing the fire in brick or tile structures, often with iron doors that could be opened. Thus came the Nuremberg stove.

The Scandinavian countries developed a type of corner fireplace of distinctive characteristics. While occupying a corner position, such a fireplace is often quite free from the wall, so that a person can walk around behind it. The hearth is raised and the massive masonry hood is supported by heavy timber lintels. At the forward corner, there is a column support, often a disused gun barrel. The hood is credited with retaining much heat.

Our interest in French fireplaces is chiefly grounded in the wealth of experimental activity in the seventeenth and eighteenth centuries, directed toward making the fireplace a more efficient heating unit. However, French mansions and chateaux participated in the ornamental phases of fireplace development, a phase of history which cannot be overlooked.

Throughout the middle ages and well into the renaissance, architects devoted their most earnest efforts to creating fireplace structures which should glorify as well as warm the noble residents of the mansions thus distinguished.

Every resource of architectural design, of painting,

sculpture and heraldry were enlisted in this type of enterprise.

Surviving examples of such fireplaces have little significance for us today, save in the matter of emphasis. They did firmly distinguish the fireplace as the focal emblem of family cohesion and home loyalty—a principle which, we trust, will never be lost to sight.

Steps in Development Fireplaces have approached their present shape or shapes by passing through the following phases. (1) The central hearth with roof outlet. (2) Hooded fireplaces with wall outlet. (3) Development of the chimney. (4) Decrease of size as coal became the prevailing fuel. (5) Reflector-like back and narrowed throat. (6) Development of the throat damper.

These steps bring us to the best current practice in the building of masonry fireplaces. But they do not, by any means, sum up all the efforts made to improve the open fire as a source of available warmth. Increasing

From the ruins of an Italian palace, this fireplace was transported to this country and reassembled.

skill in casting of iron offered inventors an inspiration to experiment in more involved shapes for the fireplace interior. Hence there came, in the seventeenth and eighteenth centuries, a flow of new suggestions in fireplace practice.

Similar ideas were embodied again and again in the conceptions of these pioneers. Three principal objects stand out—(1) Introduction of the downdraft principle, by which smoke was drawn down behind a false back or core before reaching the flue, with the presumable purpose of consuming smoke. (2) Passing air over heated surfaces and discharging it into the room, supplementing direct radiation with circulated warm air. (3) Introduction of air from outside the building to furnish oxygen for combustion and draft for discharge of the products of combustion.

Of these three innovations, the only one that has survived has been the second one mentioned. So far as we know, the first man to propose increasing the heat delivery of a fireplace by circulating heat was Louis Savot, a court physician interested in the public health problems of France. He built a fireplace in the Louvre in the early decades of the seventeenth century. He died in 1640, 66 years before Franklin was born, which interests Americans because many have the impression that the heat-circulating fireplace was first exemplified in Franklin's Pennsylvania Fireplace.

All of the many early fireplaces of this type were doomed to brief success, if any. The fact was that cast iron was a poor medium from which to fabricate the air chambers and ducts necessary in a fireplace of this type. Exposed to variable temperatures of open flame, it tended to crack or warp, letting smoke into the warm-air passage.

It was not until the development of the welding of metal plate that the principle of heat circulation became practical. Meantime a century had elapsed in which the idea had lain dormant. There are at least a half dozen brands of welded fireplace units made in the United States today.

English fireplace chronicles speak of a fireplace contrived for Prince Rupert, a cousin of King Charles II, by a mason named Bingham, that employed the downdraft principle, the smoke being drawn downward behind a false back, about half the distance to hearth level, before ascending to the flue. In starting the fire, a valve plate was provided that permitted direct ascent, the valve plate being closed when the fire was well started.

Sir John Winter is credited with being the first to introduce outdoor air as a source of draft, but the honor of first combining this ventilating feature with the principle of circulation seems to belong to a Frenchman named Gauger, who also recognized the importance of shaping the sides and back to afford the effect of a reflector. His work was publicized in 1713 in England by Desaguliers, who first applied the term "ventilation." His efforts as a promoter met little success.

A close replica of an early large fireplace with wood lintel. This shows many of the cooking facilities depended on in those days.

American Innovators

Benjamin Franklin included among his varied accomplishments a discriminating knowledge of fireplace principles, and creative ability that gave rise to the so-called Pennsylvania Fireplace, as well as the celebrated Franklin Stove, an enclosed heating device.

A long letter written by Franklin, while on shipboard returning to America, is one of the clearest expositions of fireplace principles and practice ever penned. It was written to Jan Ingenhousz, a Dutch scientist and engineer living in London.

The man who has done the most, perhaps, to shape the trend of modern fireplace practice, however, was a New Englander, born at Woburn, Massachusetts, named Benjamin Thompson. But he left America early in life and never returned. In the course of a distinguished European career, he was honored with the title of Count Rumford. Fireplaces based on principles that he expounded are known as Rumford fireplaces.

Thompson's public career was enacted in Munich, where he filled several cabinet posts and was virtual ruler of Bavaria, being given the title of Count of the Holy Roman Empire. He chose to be called Count Rumford, since Rumford, N.H. had been his most recent American home.

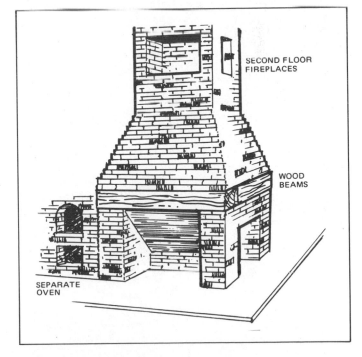

SECOND FLOOR
FIREPLACES

WOOD
BEAMS

SEPARATE
OVEN

Early American fireplace complex

English fireplace at time of Queen Victoria. Curtain at top of fireplace indicates an effort to correct a smoking tendency.

Early American; comes very close to Count Rumford standards. Note the oven at the right side.

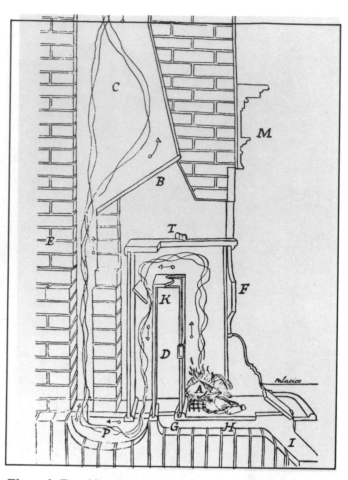

The early Franklin-designed fireplace; its many joints were its weakness.

Deeply interested in science, he returned to London after a decade and it was there that his work on fireplaces was chiefly carried out. Where other innovators had resorted much to use of iron, he relied on brick, except in the fire basket. He made fireplaces smaller and shallower than the prevailing types, with narrow back and wide flaring sides. Smoke escaped through a narrow throat placed well forward by slope of the back wall and with a rather high smoke shelf. At the height of his London experience, he mentions having some 500 smoky chimneys under his care. His fireplace designs are prized for their simplicity, fuel economy and high heat delivery.

Franklin described his Pennsylvania Fireplace in a pamphlet offered for sale in 1844. It embodies all three of the objects referred to in listing the basic aspects of the "iron age" of fireplaces—ventilation, down-draft, and heat circulation.

Fire was built in the forward chamber of the metal

Victorian Andirons—a blend of Chinese and rococo styles, were used in the White House, according to family records, during the administration of President Taylor. They are now in the Treaty Room. Copyright by White House Historical Association. Photograph by National Geographic Society

Early American taproom fireplace

unit. Heat and smoke passed over the top of a central hot-air chamber, being drawn down to a level below the level of the hearth and then discharged upward behind a false fireback of brick. The false back was connected with the fireplace breast by a sloping slab of stone or slate. Air drawn from outdoors fed the central hot-air chamber, where it was warmed and discharged through openings at the sides.

Franklin describes the advantages of heat circulation: even heat throughout the room, people warm on both sides, whether they sit near the fire or near a window. Evidence is lacking as to the number of Pennsylvania Fireplaces built in America, but we know there were some. Governor Thomas of Pennsylvania offered him a patent, but he declined as—"glad to serve others by any invention of ours"—since he had profited by the inventions of others.

The recorded history of fireplaces in the seventeenth and eighteenth centuries is chiefly the story of grand installations in the mansions of aristocrats. Consequently much more is told us about period styles and over-mantel decorations than about the working features of the fireplaces.

Such noted architects as Inigo Jones and Chris-topher Wren established standards of dignity and importance in styling which inspired scores of successors. The most talented artists, wood-carvers and cabinet makers took pride in glorifying the great halls of the English nobility with eye-compelling treatments of this focal feature.

Few of these treatments are such as we would wish to imitate today, except in watered-down form. They mark an era, however, when the open fire was still the main resource for heating.

Mantels

Early endeavour by original craftsmen to introduce definitely authentic architectural design to mantels occurred as early as 1600 A.D.

The Elizabethan period ushered in massive mantels of hand-hewn and carved stone which were focal points of the great castle halls. This style, with soaring chimney piece, continued into the Stuart period, and magnificent examples are treasured in Scotland, England and Ireland today.

English Georgian mantels of the 1700s were the first wooden mantels with architectural authenticity.

Another fireplace from Early American days. Photo courtesy of Firelands Museum, Norwalk, Ohio

Woodwork was brought from an old castle in England, wooden pegs used for fastening. Date 1590 appears below coat of arms.

Early Georgian designs were tall, proportioned for the high ceilings of great houses, and often carried elaborate carvings. They are distinguished by stately design of the overhanging mantel body, and molded step corner on the frieze.

French Louis mantels, as was the furniture of the Louis', were elegantly decorative. They introduced the classic French curve. A shell motif accentuated by fine scroll work and stately contoured pillars further emphasized the natural beauty of curving lines. The mantel shelf, similarly contoured, repeated the graceful design.

The Regency period, beginning around 1810, shows even further design refinement, with the influence of French Louis styling easily apparent.

The Victorian period, extending from 1832 to 1900, featured relatively simple mantel designs. Raised paneling effects with heavy center ornamental detail, and semicircular firebox openings, were the general rule. In the early years, cast iron Victorian mantels were used extensively throughout the British Isles.

Adam mantels, designed by Scottish architect Robert Adam in collaboration with his talented brothers, James and William, are among the most classically beautiful, and were seen in fine homes of the Victorian period. Highly decorative, they often showed a strong Greek influence with the use of the fret, lamp and scroll motifs. Marble inlay panels were features of the most highly refined designs, and carved ribbons, bows and swags were adopted.

Spanish architecture adapted and blended various styles and periods. The influence of Early English Gothic and Italian church periods is expressed clearly in many Spanish mantel designs.

Italian mantels showed the individual artisan's characteristic expression of favored romantic baroque styling.

American Colonial designs were primarily adaptations of old world periods. Some were simple stone with heavy wood slab mantel shelf supported by wood or stone corners. Later, in many of the fine homes, copies of the Grecian fluted pillar, the ribbon and shell, and other more sophisticated design details were executed by Early American cabinetmakers.

The Auxiliary Role While it is probable that better and more efficient fireplaces are being built today than at any time past, they have ceased to be the main reliance for heating. Most residences in cooler climates have provision for central heating. They have gas or electric cooking facilities.

Highly appreciated in spring and fall or other chilly periods when central plants are not in use, indispensable in extreme cold or when public utilities fail, delightful in its power to charm at any time, the fireplace remains largely an auxiliary in the practical domain of home economy.

Some form of oven for baking and roasting has ex-

The Green Room—a Federal Parlor in the White House. Empire Marble mantelpiece. Above the fireplace hangs the famous portrait of Benjamin Franklin by David Martin.

Copyright by White House Historical Association. Photograph by National Geographic Society

isted from time beyond record. Often it had an outdoor location. In other cases, it occupied a shed, apart from the residence. Such free-standing ovens generally betokened use as a utility for a neighborhood such as prevailed in colonial Virginia. Where the housewife wrestled with food preparation alone, it has been logical to make the oven a part of the fireplace. In England and in New England the term kitchen oven was used to distinguish such ovens from larger outdoor ovens or those occupying a detached shed.

Operation consisted of introducing hot coals into the oven and leaving them there until the masonry was thoroughly heated. Coals were then raked out and bread dough or other substance to be baked was introduced and the interior tightly closed until baking was complete. Similarly the oven accomplished slow roasting of meats, as an alternative to the more rapid grilling or spit roasting before an open flame.

Enthusiasm for fireplace cooking, outdoor and indoor, has restored the Dutch oven to favor as a feature of combination outdoor fireplaces and of indoor barbecues as well as those fireplaces more definitely classed as reproductions of Early American types. It should be noted, however, that the term Dutch oven has been applied in certain times, and in places, to quite different metal contrivances.

The present day modification of this historic feature is the introduction of a compact fire chamber under the oven proper, where the charcoal fire can be maintained. This fits the oven for the cooking that is not suitable to the range unit, which is usually the dominant feature of combination fireplaces.

Cooking or baking can be much more rapid with an active charcoal fire below the oven. This fire can be fed without disturbing the oven. An adequate vent is highly important. It may communicate with the main flue, or with an independent fire.

Metal parts necessary for a modern Dutch oven include the ornamental Dutch oven door, a smaller ash door and necessary grates for the support of the fire and viands being cooked. By locating the level of the charcoal grate above the floor of the fire chamber, ashes may be conveniently raked out.

For as long as mankind continues to use and enjoy the fireplace, its rich historical background will have significance. Today's home dweller, as he sits before his fireplace, establishes his most tangible link with the great ages of the past.

Present fireplace forms have grown out of forms with centuries of tradition behind them. Their stabilizing effect on an era prone to restless innovation accounts in large measure for the increasing vogue of this long established domestic institution.

The Family Dining Room on the State Floor of the White House is furnished with American pieces of the Federal Period. A gilt convex mirror crowned with an eagle hangs above the white-and-green-marble mantelpiece. Copyright by White House Historical Association. Photograph by National Geographic Society

Another Franklin fireplace inserted in conventional opening. Photo courtesy of Thomas Paine Cottage, New Rochelle, N.Y.

Planning Your Fireplace

Location Within a Room

The foremost consideration in locating the fireplace within a room is the creation of an area of comfort and repose. Needed are plenty of room for comfortable seating, and space for whatever other fireside pleasures you contemplate, such as reading, listening to music, cooking, etc. Such space is most likely to be found at the side or end of a room. The end position is very likely to be preferable on the grounds of seclusion.

In choosing the location for your fireplace, consider the traffic pattern that will evolve. Avoid placing the fireplace where traffic from door to door passes through the room between furniture and fireplace. Please consider here, also, the poor fire tender who should not be forced to trample over guests or dodge furniture when he brings in a load of fuel from the storage area.

Structural considerations in the location of the chimney will influence the placement of the fireplace. Factors that might affect the drawing capacity of the chimney and possible down-drafts are tall trees, nearby buildings, even high ground or other topographic peculiarities of the site. If you are planning to use a single chimney (separate flues, of course!) to vent the fireplace in the living room, one in the bedroom and the furnace, this will pretty well determine your fireplace location for you. You may also plan to add an outside fireplace later on off the patio and have only one or two possible patio sites.

If your house is to be built with brick rather than wood siding, it is possible to save money on brick by placing the fireplace on an outside wall. The foundation on the outside walls is already there, whereas an inside location may require more foundation. On the other hand, common brick can be used on the concealed portions of the inside fireplace, rather than expensive face brick. Anchorage is not required on chimneys wholly within the house in those areas subject to earthquake damage. Remember, too, that an inside fireplace takes up square footage in the house, while a fireplace on an outside wall does not.

Size of the Fireplace

Now, how do you go about deciding how big a fireplace, or rather fireplace opening, to have? First of all, a word of caution to over-enthusiastic fireplace buffs—a "great big fire" in a "great big fireplace" will probably drive you from the room! On the other hand, a

A spectacular fireplace in a tri-level setting creates a comfortable place to sit by the fire. Notice the feeling of warmth from the mellow hand-made tiles, exposed beams, and color of the walls in the fireplace area. Photo courtesy of Majestic

small fire in a large fireplace heats inefficiently and is less aesthetically appealing.

What we present here are certain principles that can be applied to the determination of the size of your fireplace. The main principle involved is that of fireplace "thermodynamics." There is much greater heating efficiency in a firebox thirty inches wide, well filled with flame, than there is in the same fire built in a forty-eight-inch firebox. Heat radiated from a fireplace comes, to a large extent, from the heated brickwork that surrounds the flame. Since radiant heat travels in straight lines, its effective range is limited. Therefore, plan no larger fire than the room requires, and plan the fireplace to fit the fire snugly, for maximum warmth and efficient fuel consumption.

Another principle, that of good design, requires that the size of the fireplace fit the size of the room. A fireplace that is scaled too large or too small in proportion to the size of the room is visually disturbing. Here is a table of suggested widths for fireplace openings appropriate to the size of the room.

| Size of Room | Width of Fireplace Opening in Inches | |
in Feet	in Short Wall	in Long Wall
10 × 14	24	24 to 32
12 × 16	28 to 36	32 to 36
12 × 20	32 to 36	36 to 40
12 × 24	32 to 36	36 to 48
14 × 28	32 to 40	40 to 48
16 × 30	36 to 40	48 to 60
20 × 36	40 to 48	48 to 72

The height of the fireplace opening is usually from two-thirds to three-quarters of the width. In the end, however, you must rely on your own good judgment.

Another factor to consider is the conventional wood fuel sizes available in your area. If you are going to use full-length four-foot cordwood, for example, the proportions of your fireplace will differ from one suited for half-length cordwood.

Style of Fireplaces

In planning your fireplace, one of the early considerations you must have is that of the main styles of fireplace and, out of these, which one will suit you best. By style, we are referring to the construction of the fireplace and its orientation to the room or rooms involved, not any architectural style. These main styles include the wall fireplace, the back-to-back fireplace, the corner fireplace, the two-way fireplace (through wall), the three-way fireplace, the hooded fireplace, and the free standing fireplace.

Wall Fireplace This is the most conventional style, of course, and the most frequently built. This style may incorporate the whole wall in its design or

may be a small, but dominating part of the design of the wall as a whole. Whenever possible, a wood pass-through or wood storage box should be provided.

Back-to-Back This design permits the use of the same masonry mass for two fireplaces. This is a great cost saver when there are two rooms with a common wall such as a family room and living room or patio for an outdoor fireplace and living room. However, even though two fireplaces use the same chimney, each must have a separate flue.

Corner Fireplace Corner fireplaces are of two types, inside corner and outside or projecting corner. They can be used for excellent room dividers with less danger of smoking in a cross draft.

Two-Way Fireplace This type has two opposite faces or two opposite fire openings. This style of fireplace serves as an excellent room divider and spreads its heat to both rooms on either side. Two-way, three-way, hooded, and free standing fireplaces each present separate technical problems which should be solved by the damper manufacturer.

Three-Way Fireplace This is like a peninsula, opening on three adjacent open sides and is a style that also serves as an excellent room divider, and can be very dramatic, with the fire visible on three sides.

Hooded Fireplace This type (usually with metal hood) is becoming very popular and is both dramatic and efficient. It is efficient because the metal hood is heated and gives off heat both by radiation and convection. A hooded fireplace is often less complicated to construct than the conventional form, as it sometimes permits the elimination of heavy chimney work and foundation masonry (building codes permitting). The metal hood may be of different metals (sheet iron finished in charcoal black or shiny copper, for exam-

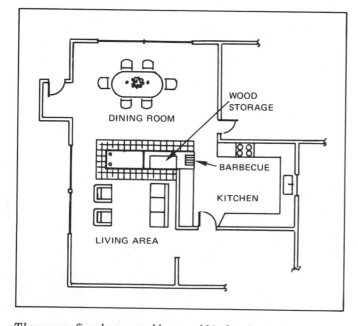

Three-way fireplace, wood box, and kitchen barbecue are all on one masonry wall.

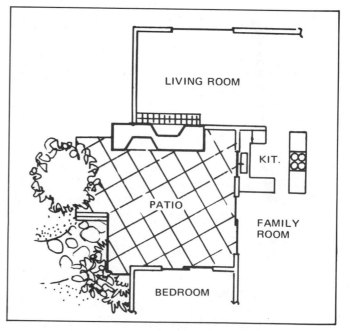

Back-to-back design economizes on masonry costs.

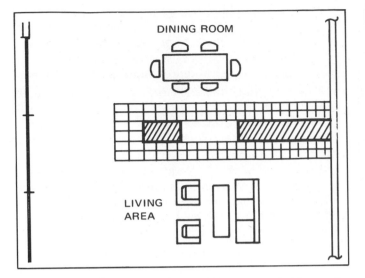

Two-way fireplace serves as excellent room divider and spreads heat and cheer to both rooms.

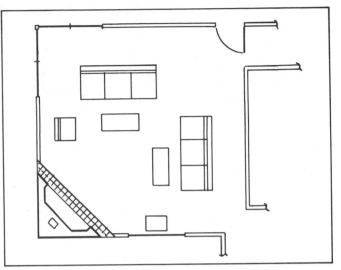

Fireplace on an inside corner with appropriate furniture arrangement.

Massive fieldstone fireplace goes beyond the glass wall and ties in the mountain view. Furniture is grouped to comple- ment both the view and the fireplace. Photo courtesy of Julius Shulman

ple) and of many different designs. The hood can increase the effectiveness of the fireplace by radiating heat when it warms up, as well as adding a striking decorative touch to the room.

Free Standing Fireplace Free-standing fireplaces are sometimes built on the same specifications as the hooded fireplaces above, but more often they are metal fireplaces. This type of fireplace permits complete freedom from the wall and allows seating on all sides of the unit.

In planning, consider also the practicality of providing for nearby wood storage. There are many ways to provide for fuel storage in a fireplace plan. A good arrangement is a fireside locker with a door that opens outside or into the garage. The wood cabinet can be integrated into the overall design of the fireplace wall. A recess can be planned in the fireplace wall for wood storage or the wood can be stacked under a raised hearth. The sight of a good supply of wood gives a sense of security and promise of long and enjoyable fires.

Ideal furniture grouping for this free standing fireplace. Photo courtesy of Lawrence Williams

Furniture Placement

There are a few general principles to remember in planning the placement of furniture around the fireplace. The main goal to keep in mind is a restful grouping of seating and tables with the fireplace as the center of interest.

Ideally the area in front of or around the hearth could be a sunken conversation pit, but, of course, this cannot always be done. What we must do instead is create an area (square, rectangular, half-circle, circle, or L-shaped) of comfort and repose. To achieve this, for example, two sofas can face each other over a low coffee table in front of the fire with two comfortable lounge chairs opposite the fireplace.

Do not forget to leave room for the business of fire tending, but not enough to allow traffic back and forth between the fireplace and furniture grouping.

The size of the furniture pieces and the grouping as a whole must be in proportion with the large mass of the fireplace. Two small arm chairs, for instance, would be lost in front of a massive fieldstone fireplace, but could be used with a smaller one.

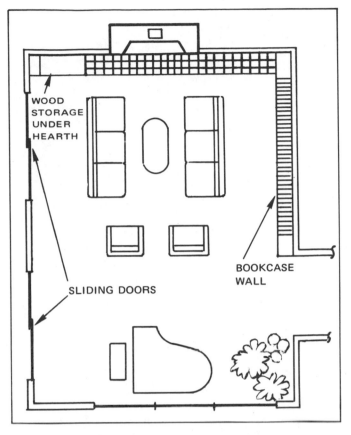

Restful furniture grouping with fireplace as center of interest.

Fireplace in window wall results in a combination of interest. Photo courtesy of California Redwood Association

A converted garage makes use of a massive fireplace for needed architectural interest. Photo courtesy of Milliken Carpets

Suspended hood over firepit provides impressive center for living/dining area with paneled staircase at right. This well-planned area includes fireplace, planting, seating and *easy-flow traffic patterns, as seen from the bird's eye view. Photo courtesy of Glen Allison*

For Appearances Sake

Now that you and your family have planned the fireplace location to meet your needs, it is time to consider the outside appearance of the fireplace front and hearth. You have decided how much you wish to emphasize the fireplace in your room, whether you wish your fireplace to dominate, or to blend in smoothly with the general decor of the room.

If your desire is the fireplace of quiet importance, that adds to the warmth and graciousness of a room without great emphasis, there are many ways of achieving this result. One method of fitting a fireplace modestly into a wall so that it is an important feature, but not the dominant one, is to pair it off with another center of attraction. A fireplace set into a storage and bookcase wall, its design being an integral part of the wall's overall design, can be very restful and pleasing. This is a particularly good combination as it puts the books close by the comfortable seating arranged facing the hearth for cozy fireside reading. Another way to blend a fireplace in with the room is to surround it with attractive wood paneling, which covers the entire wall. Setting the fireplace in the window wall is yet another interesting combination which results in a concentration of interest. An added bonus to concentrating the main focus of interest into one spot is that one seating arrangement enjoys both the view and the fire at the same time.

Facing Materials

The materials used on the fireplace front will greatly influence the impact of the fireplace upon the room. The facing may be covered with the same wood paneling that is used on the other walls of the room, or with a brick of soft tones that blends with the warm color of the wood paneling. For a dominating fireplace, a rough fieldstone facing or a shining copper hood holds the eye.

The actual construction of the fireplace makes a difference, too. A fireplace built into a masonry wall with no projections will blend right into the wall itself. If you add a contrasting cantilevered hearth and a large black metal hood, the result is eye-stopping. The ultimate example of a dramatic fireplace is a freestanding one, open on all sides with seating arranged around it.

In general, we may say that brick is not only the most popular, but also the most versatile masonry material, suitable for any style interior. The type of brick and the way it is laid, along with the overall design of the fireplace, determine whether the fireplace will be traditional or modern, formal or informal.

Clay bricks and fire seem to complement each other very well. The two types of bricks most often used are common and face brick. Common brick is rough and porous, used on inner surfaces that do not show, but sometimes used in facings for an informal effect and low cost. Face brick is a hard surfaced type used for fireplace facings and exteriors, where a more formal appearance is desired. Used bricks are another possibility; with their weathered charm they are most suitable for Early American fireplaces and other informal interiors. Roman brick, with its long shape, produces

Dramatic country club fireplace. Hearth and sidewalls are of stabilized adobe brick and the design is of glazed and fired adobe. Photo courtesy of Tidyman Studios

strong horizontal lines and is particularly effective in modern settings.

There are many other masonry materials to choose from such as fieldstone, ledge rock, sandstone, Indiana limestone, adobe, tile, marble, and attractive rocks found in a nearby riverbed or rock pile on your lot. The choice depends on your own preference, on the overall architecture of the house, or on the textures and colors needed in one particular room.

Wood paneling is another pleasing and popular material for the fireplace facing. A wood paneled wall adds warmth and textural interest to a room. The colors and textures of wood and masonry complement each other and are good in combination.

The wood wall may be in the style of formal Colonial paneling or may be rough barn-siding surrounding a large Early American hearth. A den seems to call for masculine pine-paneled walls, whereas redwood is particularly suitable for modern interiors, where it adds warmth to the sleek design.

There is a set of safety standards for fireplace facing which concerns the use of any combustible material such as wood trim or paneling. There should be 3½″

minimum clearance on all sides of the fireplace opening. If the wood projects more than 1½″ at the top of the opening, then the minimum clearance should be 12 inches at that point. Check your local code about this, as requirements differ across the country.

Hearth

The fireplace hearth is, basically, a rectangle of masonry or other fireproof material laid in front of the fireplace opening to protect the floor from sparks and the heat of the fire. The materials used and the design of the hearth, however, play an important part in the appearance of your fireplace.

The hearth may be flush with the floor, raised, or cantilevered. The floor level hearth can be spread over more of an area than simply that required for safety. It may extend out to enclose the whole seating area or may even be recessed below floor level to dramatize the fireplace and its surrounding space. The raised hearth serves to bring the fireplace up to an intimate height and is especially good for bedrooms, dining rooms and dens. The space under the raised hearth

Carefully crafted wood paneling above white brick fireplace, with raised hearth and wood storage compartment, accents study area. Photo courtesy of Ed Dull

Excellent use of brick in large projecting fireplace and walls of living room. Photo courtesy of Herrlin Studio

may be filled in with masonry or could provide convenient wood storage. If the raised hearth is long enough, cushions may be placed on it for informal seating.

The cantilevered hearth is an excellent way to dramatize the fireplace and may project out quite far and extend the whole length of the fireplace wall for a really striking design. The use of a contrasting material for the hearth adds to the dramatic effect of the strong horizontal line.

The front fireplace hearth should extend 8 inches on each side of the fireplace opening and 16 inches out in front for minimum safety requirements. Again, you should check with your local codes on this.

Mantels

The mantel of the fireplace was one of the working parts when the fireplace was depended upon to cook the family's meals. It served as a warming shelf and could hold pots and seasonings. Later on, when the fireplace moved from the kitchen into the living room, the mantel was used primarily for decorative purposes. The style of the mantel was in keeping with the architectural style of the house and the mantelpiece became a display shelf for treasured family heirlooms.

Some contemporary designers have omitted the mantel entirely, preferring instead to keep only the

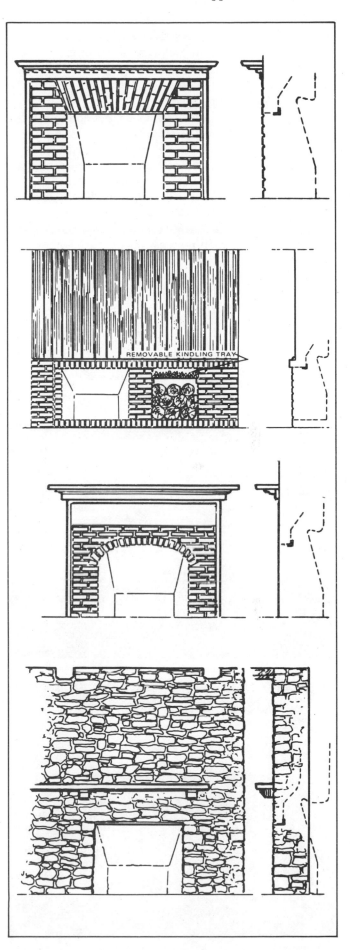

Slate hearth cantilevered over wood storage and duplicate lower hearth. Photo courtesy of Joseph Molitor

essential features of the fireplace. Sometimes, however, the mantel is used as a device to tie in the fireplace with the architectural elements of the room.

Mantels are usually made of wood and they can be carpenter-made on the job or purchased ready-made from millwork houses.

There are many classical styles of wood mantels to choose from. You may select from the elaborate curved carving of a French or Victorian mantelpiece to the classic refinement of detail of an Adam mantel, to the simple proportions of an Early American mantel. A heavy slab of wood set in a rough fieldstone fireplace may be suitable for a vacation home.

The design of the mantel should be planned carefully so that it is in keeping with the overall design of the hearth as it is a very effective decorative element. The wooden mantel may be painted to match the wall covering or the natural wood of the mantel may be finished to match the wood paneling in the room. In remodeling a room, a new mantel can be most effective and could help to update the fireplace or to change the feeling of the old fireplace entirely. The same safety restrictions mentioned earlier apply again here to the mantel.

A group of mill-built mantels from various periods. Photos courtesy of Endeavour Periods, Inc.

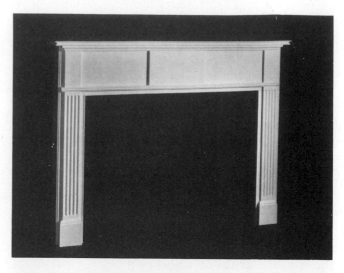

Hoods

The fireplace hood can be the most striking feature of the hearth. The hood, of course, is not only decorative, but can increase the effectiveness of the fireplace by radiating heat when it is warmed up.

Fireplace hoods may be made of metal, plaster, or even masonry. The metals most often used are copper (polished, natural warm reddish tone, or oxidized green), aluminum and stainless steel, or steelplate painted charcoal black. The metal in the hood may be textured for added interest by hammering, sandblasting, etching, or polishing. Plaster hoods are made over a metal frame that covers the flue.

The shape of the hood adds to the feeling of warmth and interest which a fireplace brings to a room. There are some traditional shapes for fireplace hoods or they may be freely designed to suit your individual needs. They may project from a fireplace wall or hang over a free-standing hearth.

Furnishings and Accessories

The selection of furnishings and accessories for the fireplace deserves some time and thought. You may select them for purely utilitarian reasons or for ornamentation, hopefully a happy combination of both. Problems of size, proportion, and general appropriateness will have to be considered. Whatever is decided is likely to affect your pleasure in using your fireplace and is fairly permanent in nature besides. Remind yourself, when making your selections, that the important thing is the fire itself and that you are trying to enhance the looks of the fireplace, not overpower it.

To carry and hold fuel, a coal hod or wood carrier, or both, will be needed. To support the burning fuel, fire basket, andirons, and log rest are the choices. To start the fire, perhaps a fire lighter will be needed. Tongs, log fork, and shovel feed the fire. A poker stirs it and a bellows may be useful in stimulating the flame.

This imaginative fireplace screens living room from entrance foyer of house. Photo courtesy of Julius Shulman

A two-story space, opening to mezzanine bedroom area, utilizes hanging hood over aggregate-floored hearth. Photo courtesy of Julius Schulman

Pine paneled wall with bookcases has mantel of same material.

Poker, tongs, log fork, brush and shovel are usually purchased in matched sets with a support of matching design or hung and a bracket fastened to the masonry. For a useful fireplace, select carefully for its utility as well as attractiveness. Many are made for appearances only and are not of adequate size or weight, or the handles may not have a good grip. There are many different designs available to match the style or design of your fireplace, available in brass, steel, and black finishes.

The choice of the fire basket or grate involves the question of size. A small basket in the middle of a large hearth presents a faulty appearance and also sacrifices warmth, since the flame does not reach and heat the surrounding brickwork enough to give back radiant heat. There are several designs available in fire baskets, making it possible to suit your fireplace. Some of the designs are adaptable to either coal or wood.

Where wood is the dominant fuel, and especially in larger fireplaces, a pair of heavy log rests afford the proper support. The heaviest log that is likely to be put in a fireplace will not warp these supports if they are good and sturdy.

Andirons are made in an infinite variety of shapes and sizes. The andiron represents a tradition that goes back to the earliest days of domestic fires, and originally was equipped with hooks and projections for the support of a spit or rod, from which other utensils were suspended. Modern use of the andirons is mostly for ornamentation. When choosing andirons, select for suitable design and proper size. Most log rests, grates and fire baskets are designed so that the shank of an andiron will rest beneath, preserving the ornamental value of the andiron post even when other devices are bearing the fire load.

The firescreen is another valuable accessory to the fireplace. The basic types of firescreens include folding doors of tempered glass; standing screens that require no installation; and attached screens, mounted either outside or flush with the opening. Decide how you want your fireplace to look when it isn't being used—then you can be sure it will give you enjoyment when it is in use.

An oversized screen can make the fireplace seem much larger than it is and this may be desirable for the overall balance between the fireplace and the room. In addition to black and brass, other colors are available in screens and may be used to complement the scheme. Screens should be used to add to the appearance of a fireplace so it would be a mistake to use an ornate screen on a fireplace that is well designed and harmonizes with the room. Conversely, a screen may be used to conceal or modify a poorly designed fireplace.

The need for some type of screen stems from the danger of flying sparks. When fuel is used which tends to snap, such as cannel coal or some kinds of resinous woods, or when small children are playing in front of the fire, the screen should be used continuously. Also, for obvious reasons, the fireplace should always be screened if it is left to burn itself out when the family retires.

Conventional Fireplaces

The conventional masonry fireplace has become the standard in America—by being suitable to our needs; adaptable to our fuels of wood or coal; moderate in cost, or elaborately expensive to suit the variable needs or desires; enjoyable in home, cottage, camp, club, office or mansion; as a main source of heat and comfort or, in buildings with central heat, as a supplemental or emergency heat source, and, in all cases providing the nostalgic, heart-warming pleasures of a blazing log fire.

Planning the location, size, and general character of your fireplace is a subject worthy of careful study by architects, builders, homeowners, and masons.

Home planners often need to be warned against the sentimental desire for "a great big fireplace." They forget that a great big fire would probably drive them out of the room. They need to be told that a small fire in a big fireplace is not efficient heating.

As mentioned earlier, a fireplace thirty inches wide, well filled with flame, will provide more heat than the same fire built in a larger fireplace.

Heat radiated from a fireplace comes, to a large extent, from the heated brickwork that surrounds the flame. The closer the brickwork to the flame, the more it is heated. In the case of the thirty-inch fireplace in the diagram, the back and sides are both heated. In the forty-eight-inch fireplace, only a portion of the back masonry is heated. More heat undoubtedly goes up the chimney.

The larger fireplace requires a larger flue. In case of the forty-eight-inch opening, the flue lining would have to be the sixteen-inch-by-sixteen-inch size, while the smaller, thirty-inch fireplace would be adequately served by a twelve-inch-by-twelve-inch flue. To maintain a steady draft, the large flue would need 50 percent more air from some source. With a moderate-size fire, it probably would not get such a volume of air. The up-draft would tend to be sluggish and, if ventilation were restricted, there would be a tendency to down-draft. And, presuming that a good draft were established in the larger flue, there would plainly be more cold air to heat.

So, plan no larger fire than your room requires, and plan the fireplace to fit the fire snugly if you want maximum warmth.

Plans

If carefully tested plans such as those shown in this book are used, or the fireplace is built in accord with the tables and technical standards provided, the operation should be completely satisfactory. Where trouble is encountered it will be found to be caused by some environmental condition or the violation of the basic rules found herein.

Materials

Brick, concrete block, stone and adobe may be used in fireplace construction. Hollow concrete block should only be used in the foundation and ashpit areas. Fire brick, soapstone, or other refractory material must be used to line the firebox, and fire brick or flue tile should be used for the inner course of the flue.

Steel fireplace lining, at least one-fourth inch thick, may be used instead of fire brick. Installation should be in accordance with manufacturers' recommendations.

Mortar Setting fire brick and parging in smoke chamber—use fire clay mortar (refractory mortar). Masonry mortar should not be used for parging.

Flue lining—use fire clay mortar or type M or S. (Table) All other mortar shall be type S or N. Mortar should be used within two and a half hours of mixing. Calcium chloride may be added to accelerate setting and hardening in winter weather only in an amount not to exceed one percent by weight of the Portland

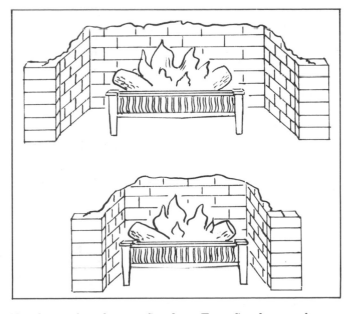

Handicap of too large a fireplace. Top—fireplace too large for fire. Radiates less heat than where flame fits the fireplace smoothly—as bottom.

Chimney Cap
Available precast for some standard flue sizes or cast in place. Note that the liner projects through the cap several inches.

Flue and Flue Lining
The area of the flue should equal one-twelfth to one-eighth the area of the opening of the fireplace (width times height). Lining is supported on masonry.

Smoke Chamber
Together with the smoke shelf, this area is important to a smoke-free fire. Both sides slope to the flue and it is important that they slope identically, otherwise the fire will burn on one side of the firebox only.

The entire smoke chamber and smoke shelf is parged with fire clay mortar (refractory mortar) or type "S" mortar one-half inch thick.

Throat and Damper
These parts are usually one and the same. The damper is capable of being opened and closed gradually to control the draft and keep out cold air when the fireplace is not in use. The opening in square inches should be at least 90% of that required for the flue.

Firebox
This is the area that comes alive with dancing flames and gleaming embers. To do this the firebox must be correctly proportioned, sealed, vented, and well constructed.

Hearth
The inner hearth is that portion within the fire area and is usually built of fire brick but may be other types of hard brick, concrete, stone, tile or other non-combustible heat-resistant materials. The outer hearth is built of the same type materials and should extend a minimum of eight inches on each side of the fireplace opening and sixteen inches in front. (Note: These figures are twelve inches and eighteen inches in areas covered by the Uniform Building Code.)

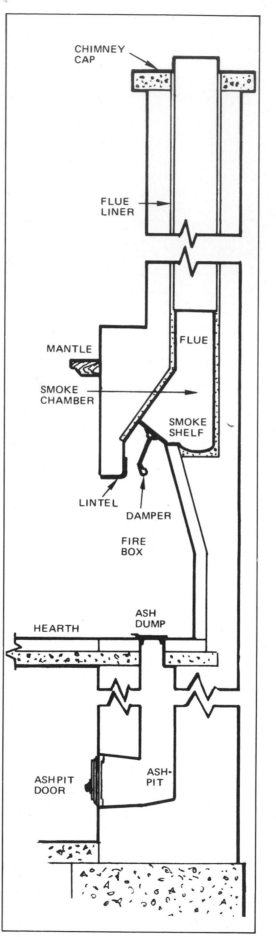

Smoke Shelf
This is a horizontal shelf, usually concave and extending backward from the rear of the throat or damper to the rear flue wall. It directs cold air downdrafts which are present in the early stages of the fire, causing them to eddy and drift upward with the rising air currents.

Ashpit
This is the hollow space below the hearth into which ashes fall through the ash dump door located in the hearth. A metal door is provided in the ashpit for the occasional removal of ashes. In basementless homes, particularly those built on a concrete slab, it may not be feasible to provide an ashpit unless the hearth has been raised. In this case the ashpit door faces outside.

Foundation
Consult your local building code, since these codes differ according to existing soil and moisture conditions in individual areas. If total weight is needed to compute the depth and rise of the foundation required, figure brick at 130 lbs. and concrete at 150 lbs. per cubic foot. For cubic footage, figure the entire cross section volume including the open portion of the flue and firebox. The footing should extend at least below the depth of the greatest frost penetration.

As a general rule, footings should be of concrete at least twelve inches thick and should extend at least six inches on all sides of the foundation. Concrete should be poured on undisturbed soil.

Foundation walls should be a minimum of eight inches thick.

This antique brick fireplace wall continues into the stairway. Raised hearth and arched lintel are of the same material. The furniture arrangement and warm color create a welcoming and comfortable gathering place. Photo courtesy of Hedrich-Blessing

Strong structural beams accent lines of the soffit and bring out the rich grain of the paneling judiciously used in this family room. The weathered wood paneling uses interesting application with horizontal lines. Photo courtesy of Georgia Pacific

The gleaming copper hood, raised hearth and mellow used-brick fireplace front (upper right) combine to make this inglenook a cozy gathering place. Photo courtesy of Hedrich-Blessing

Upward movement of fireplace and chimney provides a symmetrical center of interest in this sleek and sophisticated California living room. Note the raised ceramic tile hearth. Photo courtesy of Glen Allison

This Colonial family room has a used brick fireplace that blends well with the weathered wood paneling and cabinets. Photo courtesy of Vermont Weatherboard

This elegant fireplace wall (upper right) was created with "travel panels." Panels framed with wood molding were painted to simulate Colonial paneling in this remodeled living room. Photo courtesy of Western Wood Moulding

This traditionally designed freestanding wood stove (lower right) is functional as well as an integral part of the room design. Heat from the stove complements the conventional heating system. Photo courtesy of Ashley

The paneled wall and fireplace mantel work give this room its focus. Use of paneling and molding from the local store created the traditional look of priceless restored architectural detailing. Traditional furnishings are naturally grouped to dramatize the hearth.

This modern family room addition incorporates a copperplated freestanding fireplace as the focal point of the room. Photo courtesy of Georgia Pacific

The freestanding porcelain-enameled metal fireplace creates a congenial area for this sophisticated modern apartment interior. Photo courtesy of Majestic Fireplaces

This custom-built freestanding fireplace balances exquisite view through the window wall. Wood storage is provided under white plastic laminate bench. Note interesting arrangement on fireplace wall. Photo courtesy of Glen Allison

Both heat and fireplace cheer are provided for this well-finished and decorated barn by this freestanding unit from Norway. Door opens for fireplace use, or closes tight for maximum heating efficiency. Photo courtesy of Kristia Associates

The black metal freestanding fireplace brings a crackling woodburning fire to this small vacation home. Photo courtesy of Majestic Fireplaces

This efficient heat circulating fireplace heats the living room in this remodeled log cabin. Used-brick fireplace wall includes barbecue and wood storage, with a hearth raised to seating height. Photo courtesy of Hedrich-Blessing

Accent wall of rich brown tile sets off both the warm wood walls and the light ceiling. Photo courtesy of American Olean

A prebuilt metal fireplace in an interesting two-way projecting corner installation saves space and can be added to the appropriate room. The fire is visible all around the corner. Notice the well-chosen fireplace accessories. Photo courtesy of Heatilator Fireplaces

This corner fireplace was added to this den/recreation room to provide a warmer, well designed environment. The extended hearth provides good storage space. Photo courtesy of Majestic Fireplaces

A massive used-brick fireplace can be the focal point of a large family room. Red-wood planks enhance the vertical design of this fireplace. Photo courtesy of Majestic

This colorful ceramic tile interior patio barbecue is vented with color-matched metal hood. Photo courtesy of American Olean

This black slate fireplace wall (upper right) complements modern interior and exciting exterior view. Photo courtesy of Hedrich-Blessing

An interesting design (lower right) that gives a freestanding feeling to the large brick fireplace. Note the good wood storage provided and the drama of the chimney viewed through the window. Photo courtesy of Hedrich-Blessing

Here the fireplace has been incorporated into the bookcase wall. Notice the beautiful simplicity and good proportions of the design of the wall as a whole. Photo courtesy of Hedrich-Blessing

This built-in fireplace unit is one of the most energy efficient units available on the market. Smoke is released and heat circulated back into the room. Photo courtesy of Majestic Fireplaces

This fieldstone fireplace and hearth with built-in wood storage seem just right with deck and view beyond. The blue-green accent of the upholstery pieces particularly enhances the wood area-stove. Photo courtesy of Hedrich-Blessing

Exciting combination of textures and interesting built-in seating form an inviting fireplace in this comfortable family room. Photo courtesy of Charles R. Pearson

The mellow brick fireplace is a strong architectural element in this beautiful interior. Note the interesting interplay of lines, planes, colors and textures. Photo courtesy of Herrlin Studios

Cement. It should be added in solution as part of mixing water.

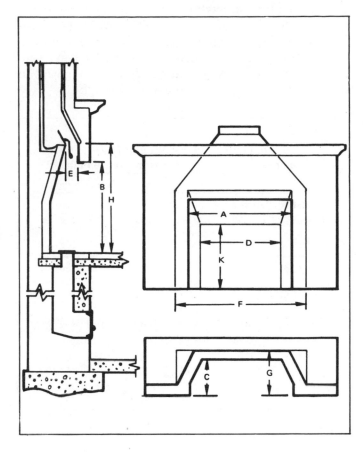

Mortar Mix				
Mortar type	Portland cement or Portland blast furnace slag cement	Hydrated lime or lime putty	Type II masonry cement	Aggregate
M	1	¼	—	3 to 3¾
	1	—	1	4½ to 6
S	1	¼ to ½	—	3¼ to 4½
	½	—	1	3¼ to 4½
N	1	½ to 1	—	4 to 6
	—	—	1	2¼ to 3

Flue Lining   The lining should be clay tile manufactured in accordance with ASTM C-315-56. Thickness increases with size from a minimum of ⅝″ to 1⅝″ for the twenty-four-inch-by-twenty-four-inch size.

Three different methods of measurement are employed for the three types of flue lining: outside measurement for the old standard; "nominal" outside

Dimensions											
Finished Opening											
A	B	C	D	E	F	G	H	K	Standard Flue Lining	Modular Flue Lining	
Width	Height	Depth	Back	Throat	Width	Depth	Smoke Shelf Height	Vertical Back			
24	28	16	16	9	30	20	32	14	8½ × 8½	8 × 12	
26	28	16	18	9	32	20	32	14	8½ × 8½	8 × 12	
28	28	16	20	9	34	20	32	14	8½ × 13	12 × 12	
30	30	16	22	9	36	20	34	15	8½ × 13	12 × 12	
32	30	16	24	9	38	20	34	15	8½ × 13	12 × 12	
34	30	16	26	9	40	20	34	15	8½ × 13	12 × 12	
36	31	18	27	9	42	22	36	16	13 × 13	12 × 16	
38	31	18	29	9	44	22	36	16	13 × 13	12 × 16	
40	31	18	31	9	46	22	36	16	13 × 13	12 × 16	
42	31	18	33	9	48	22	36	16	13 × 13	12 × 16	
44	32	18	35	9	50	22	37	17	13 × 13	12 × 16	
46	32	18	37	9	52	22	37	17	13 × 13	12 × 16	
48	32	20	38	9	54	24	37	17	13 × 18	16 × 20	
50	34	20	40	9	56	24	39	18	13 × 18	16 × 20	
52	34	20	42	9	58	24	39	18	13 × 18	16 × 20	
54	34	20	44	9	60	24	39	18	13 × 18	16 × 20	
56	36	20	46	9	62	24	41	19	18 × 18	20 × 20	
58	36	22	47	9	64	26	41	19	18 × 18	20 × 20	
60	36	22	49	9	66	26	41	19	18 × 18	20 × 20	

dimensions for the modular standard; and the inside diameter for the round linings. Whatever type of lining is used, the sectional areas provide a guide for the desired flue capacity, which should be based on a sectional area not less than one-tenth or one-eighth the flue area, depending on the chimney height.

Flue Liner Dimensions and Areas Dimensions in inches—Areas in square inches					
Standard Liners		Modular Liners		Round Liners	
Outside Dimensions	Area of Passage	Nominal Outside Dimensions	Area of Passage	Inside Diameter	Area of Passage
8½ × 8½	52.56	8 × 12	57	8	50.26
		8 × 16	74		
8½ × 13	80.50			10	78.54
		12 × 12	87		
8½ × 18	109.69	12 × 16	120	12	113.00
13 × 13	126.56	16 × 16	162	15	176.70
13 × 18	182.84	16 × 20	208	18	254.40
18 × 18	248.06	20 × 20	262	20	314.10
		20 × 24	320	22	380.13
		24 × 24	385	24	452.30

Metal Parts These should be of approved manufacture. Dampers must have the ability to close the throat effectively and the opening should be adjustable by rotary face control, poker, or chain control. Damper should extend the width of the firebox and when open have an area equal to 90 percent of the required flue area. High formed dampers are available which incorporate the throat construction and, be-cause of their extra height and width, allow a shallower fireplace. Without the need to construct a throat of brick and mortar, labor costs are reduced. Consult manufacturer's literature.

Special dome dampers incorporating damper, smoke chamber, and lintel are available for multi-opening fireplaces. When used, the fireplace should be built in accordance with the manufacturer's literature covering the dome.

Design

A great deal of the satisfaction to be gained from a conventional masonry fireplace will depend on adherence to proper proportioning of the opening, throat, flue, etc. Many of the recommended dimensions and proportions used in fireplacing vary from source to source and from building code to code. What we attempt to do here is to present a consensus. If these rules are followed, you should have a successful fireplace.

Dimensions
   Width—24" to 84" opening
   Height—⅔ to ¾ of the width
   Depth—½ to ⅔ of the height
   Flue Area—FHA requirements are:
   Area of the flue:
   • one-tenth of the area of fireplace opening for chimneys fifteen feet in height or over.
   • one-eighth of area of fireplace opening for chimneys under fifteen feet in height.
   • Corner fireplaces or fireplaces open on two or more sides should be designed for each specific installation.

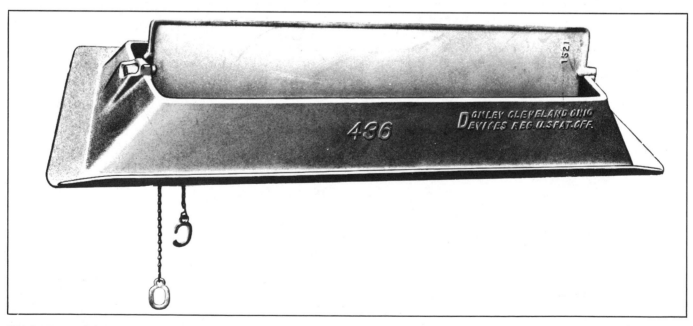

Chain control damper

- Height of chimney is measured from fireplace throat to top.
- The above is for rectangular flues lined with flue lining or fire brick.
- At altitudes over 2000 feet the area of the flue and the height of the chimney should be increased 5 percent for each 1000 feet of elevation. Check with local building official.

Multiple Opening Fireplaces These fireplaces can be built so as to be useful and enjoyable and so as to contribute to the decor of the room or rooms on which they face, but they are not exempt from the general principles of construction that govern all successful fireplaces. As with regular wall-type fireplaces, the size of openings should be in proportion to the size of the room. These fireplaces are of three types: corner, two- and three-way fireplaces.

In determining the flue area, you must count the area of each open face. The drawing and table shows the areas recommended by the Federal Housing Administration. Dampers used are usually of a special type and fireplaces should be built in accordance with the damper manufacturer's instructions.

Corner Fireplaces These fireplaces should have a sloping back wall like conventional fireplaces. The open end of this fireplace (around the corner from the principal face) can have a short wall, four inches to eight inches, to act as a baffle in the event of cross-drafts. This is particularly desirable in the event the fireplace juts into the room like a peninsula.

Corner fireplaces can be built without a supporting corner post by use of specially designed lintels to cantilever the brick work around the corner.

Two-Way Double Opening Fireplaces These are located in a chimney stack that serves as a partition. By building one fire you cheer and warm two rooms. Care should be taken that potential cross-drafts such as a front and a rear door in line with the firebox do not spread smoke and ashes into one of the rooms.

Three-Way Fireplace This fireplace can be a peninsula like the corner fireplace and part of a room dividing masonry mass, or it can project from a sidewall into the room. In effect, this fireplace would bring the fire into the center of the family circle. As in the corner fireplace, short walls are sometimes a safeguard against smoking.

Air Supply for Combustion It takes air to run a fireplace—air for draft, oxygen for combustion. In homes of past generations this was sometimes supplied overabundantly. The roaring logs drew drafts through every chink and cranny of window or door. Chairs with wings at the level of the face were provided to keep off drafts from the rear, while the face and shins toasted.

Until recent times there has been little difficulty in securing the moderate up-draft needed for the operation of the present-day fireplace. But newer tech-

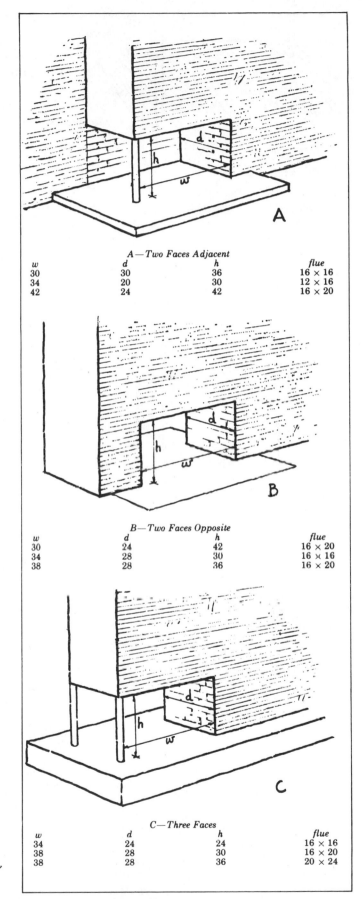

A—Two Faces Adjacent

w	d	h	flue
30	30	36	16 × 16
34	20	30	12 × 16
42	24	42	16 × 20

B—Two Faces Opposite

w	d	h	flue
30	24	42	16 × 20
34	28	30	16 × 16
38	28	36	16 × 20

C—Three Faces

w	d	h	flue
34	24	24	16 × 16
38	28	30	16 × 20
38	28	36	20 × 24

Flue areas for fireplaces having 2 or more openings (faces). Photo courtesy of Federal Housing Administration

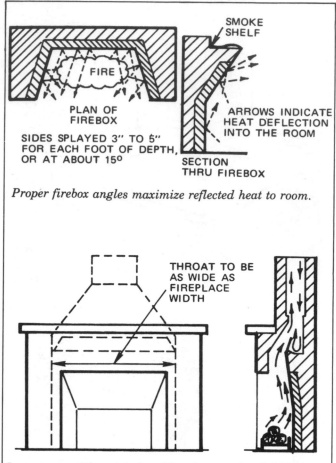

Proper firebox angles maximize reflected heat to room.

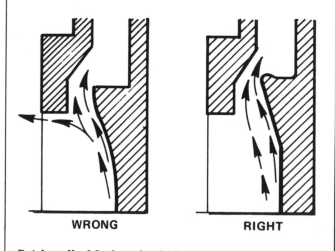

Importance of throat design. Note how smoke shelf deflects down drafts, causing them to mix with hot gases and go back up the flue.

Brick wall of firebox should be angular, not curved.

niques of weatherstripping and caulking and the use of special gaskets on casement windows have made many a modern interior tight as a drum. Furthermore, if a furnace or an incinerator is operating, the only source from which they can get needed combustion air is down the fireplace chimney. The down-draft that this creates prevents maintaining a fire on the hearth. Even if there is no other fire in the interior, perfect tightness can prevent the building of a satisfactory open fire.

The solution to all these problems is ventilated interiors. The slight opening of a basement window, if there is no other ventilating device, will generally provide the air needed for the fireplace, furnace, and incinerator. Another solution is to install a special ventilating brick between the outside and the ashpit. This will supply air through the ash dump for the fire.

Shape of the Fireplace   For maximum heat radiation, the sides of the fireplace should be splayed three to five inches for each foot of depth or about 15 degrees. The back wall should not be built on a vertical curve as it may encourage smoke to enter the room. The wall should have a vertical portion (see table) and then slope forward to the throat. The ash dump should be located under the fire.

Where a cheerful fireplace without maximum heat is desired, the firebox may be rectangular in shape, as wide in the rear as in the front. Heat can be further minimized by a larger flue and damper.

Throat-Smoke Chamber   The throat of the fireplace should always be as wide as the firebox is wide and from four to five inches in depth. Modern dampers (drawing) are constructed to combine the damper and the throat which automatically insures this detail of construction.

The back edge of the damper should always rest on the forward edge of the smoke shelf. The joint between the damper and the bottom of the smoke shelf should be sealed with mortar so that flames can only reach the flue through the damper throat. Ends of the damper should be installed to permit expansion from heat.

A great deal of care should be taken to see that

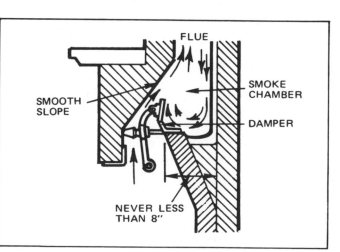

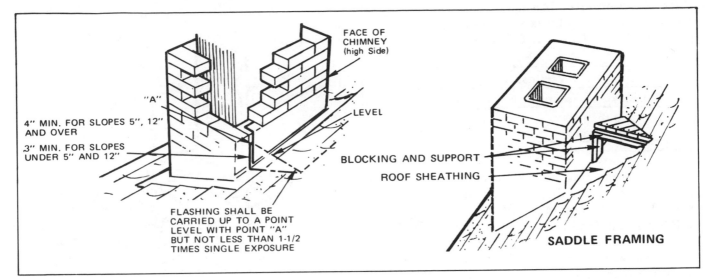

Flashing for chimneys thirty inches in width or less where no saddle is required.

Chimney flashing and saddle (cricket) framing details.

proper dimensions are maintained in the smoke chamber; that the front of the wall is not drawn in so abruptly as to interfere with the rising smoke, and that all surfaces are smooth and free from large projections.

Chimney

Each fireplace should have a separate flue.

The chimney should extend at least two feet above any part of a roof, ridge, or parapet wall within ten feet of the chimney. This should be three feet on flat roofs.

All fireplace chimneys should have flue lining except when chimney walls are at least eight inches nominal thickness.

Chimney connectors (smoke pipes) where used to connect metal fireplaces to masonry chimneys should have a maximum length of ten feet or 75 percent of the vertical height of the chimney, whichever is the lesser. A thimble (metal or clay form in chimney to receive smoke pipe) should be used.

Unequal projection of two or more flues in the same chimney is a safeguard against smoke pouring out one flue and down the other.

Proximity of a tree or high building may interfere with the free flow of smoke. The remedy is often found in hooding as shown here.

Chimneys should be flashed and counter-flashed with corrosion resistant metal where they penetrate the roof. A cricket or saddle should be used on the high side of a sloping roof to shed the water around the chimney. (Basis—FHA 902-7 P. 163)

A chimney cap should be provided of concrete or other non-combustible material. Cap should be sloped from flue to outside edge with a minimum thickness of 2 inches. No masonry mortar should be used for this purpose.

Spark screens are desirable if the location is in a wooded area or close to flammables. Rust resistant wire mesh having openings from one-half inch to five-eighths of an inch is used. Top of the screen should be at least twelve inches above the chimney cap.

Clearances Fireplace and chimney walls should be separated from combustible material as follows: Framing members, two-inch airspace. Airspace should be fire-stopped at floor level with extension of ceiling finish, strips of asbestos board or other non-combustible material. Subfloor and flooring—three-quarter-inch airspace.

Surround Combustible material should not be within three and one-half inches of the sides of a fireplace opening. Combustible material above (mantel) and projecting more than 1½ inches in front of the fireplace opening shall be placed at least twelve inches above the opening.

Reinforcement In earthquake areas masonry chimneys and fireplaces should be reinforced and anchored to the frame as follows:

Vertical Bars		
Chimney Area (sq. in.)	No. of Bars	Size of Bar
Less than 300	4	No. 3
300 or over	4	No. 4

Install reinforcing full height of chimney, hooked into footing and chimney cap. Unless joints are welded, bars shall be installed without splices.

Reinforcing should be placed at corners of chimney in mortar joints between inner and outer course of eight-inch walls or installed in two inches of cement grout between masonry and flue lining.

Horizontal Bars No. 2 bars, twenty-four inches o.c. embedded in mortar joints, and No. 3 bars at chimney cap and each plane of anchorage.

Anchorage Anchor chimneys which are entirely or partly outside of exterior walls to structures at each floor line six feet or more above grade and at the upper ceiling or roof line.

Anchorage should consist of one-quarter-inch steel straps or equivalent reinforcing bars anchored to chimney masonry and to structural members of framework.

Construction

Two methods are generally used. In the first, the rough brickwork is completed from foundation to chimney top, leaving the construction of the firebox, hearth, smoke chamber, and chimney face for later, after the roof is on the building and more skilled hands are available. In the second method (more efficient), the fireplace is nearly completed as the work progresses, possibly leaving only the surround and outer hearth to be completed later. Either method will produce a successful fireplace.

Construction should follow detailed plans provided by the architect or fireplace equipment manufacturer.

Hearth The hearth can be built on a reinforced concrete slab cantilevered out from the fireplace to support the outer hearth. This makes the hearth completely independent of the floor construction. In a variation of this, the outer hearth is supported by a brick arch springing from the foundation wall. Where the cantilever method is used, one-half-inch steel reinforcing bars form a grid ten to twelve inches on center. The steel should be about one inch from the top of the 3½-inch slab and the slab is keyed into the back wall of the fireplace. Combustible forms and centering should be removed.

A slab may also be constructed with brick and mortar. Ribbed metal lath serves as the form and is laid in

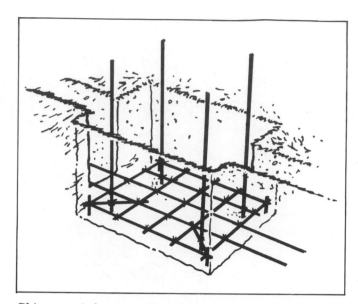

Chimney reinforcement is tied into footing bars.

the mortar on top of the brick walls of the chimney base and supported at the projecting end by a temporary form.

On the metal lath is placed a bed of type M mortar deep enough to cover the ribs. This is followed at once by the placement of the brick on edge one-half inch apart without mortar. The joints should then be filled with cement mortar grout and the reinforcing bars set in place, pressing them down into position about one and one-half inches below the top surface.

Another simpler method is used in some parts of the country. "T" irons are used to support brick which constitutes the sub-hearth. The "T" irons rest on the front foundation wall and then on a 2 × 4 ledger nailed to the face of the header in the fireplace opening. Although this method relies to some small extent on the support of the outer hearth from the floor joist, we have never seen an unsatisfactory installation of this type, and it is far less expensive.

Firebox Fire brick is laid in fire clay mortar with a maximum joint thickness of one-fourth inch. When laid the two-inch way (on edge) the firebox will need to be eight inches thick. Without the fire brick it should be twelve inches thick.

Fire brick and facing brick should be tied to rough masonry with galvanized steel brick ties.

Flue Lining First flue liner should be supported by a ledge provided in masonry at the top of the smoke chamber.

Flue lining should be installed ahead of the construction of the chimney so it is carried up, carefully bedding one on the other in mortar with close fitting joints left smooth on the inside.

Where two flues adjoin each other in the same chimney, stagger joints at least seven inches or install wythe (four-inch course of brick bonded into chimney walls).

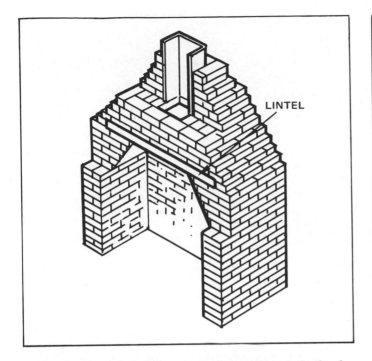

Method of building a fireplace where firebox is built after chimney construction. Note lintel over smoke chamber and support for breast lintel to be installed later. With this method of construction, the entire fireplace front may be torn out at some future date for remodeling without endangering the structure. Note also the support for the flue lining.

Where more than two flues are located in the same chimney, install a four-inch wythe bonded into the chimney separating flues into groups of one or two.

Where diagonal offsets are necessary in flue lining, bevel the edges of the liner at change in direction to insure smooth, tight joints.

Chimney Offset Masonry chimneys may be offset at a slope of not more than four inches in twenty-four inches but not more than one-third of the dimension of the chimney in the direction of the offset.

Changes in size or shape of chimneys should not be made within a distance of six inches above or below roof joists or rafters. It is sometimes desirable to increase the size of the chimney before it penetrates the roof line, for aesthetic reasons. Dummy flues are often provided in the enlarged chimney.

Hooded Fireplaces

Metal hoods add drama, and because the metal is heated and radiates heat into the room, they often increase heating efficiency.

Some hooded fireplaces are simply disguised conventional fireplaces with decorative metal over the opening. The standards of flue area, etc., given earlier apply to these fireplaces.

Other hooded fireplaces require special design by a competent fireplace designer or one of the manufacturers of custom hoods. Although the same principles

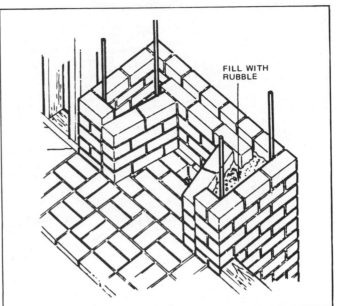

Reinforcement bars at firebox level.

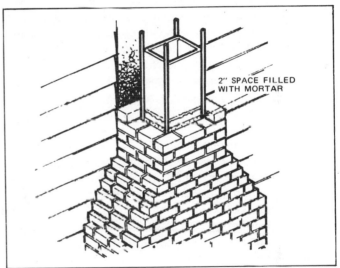

Reinforcing bars at flue level.

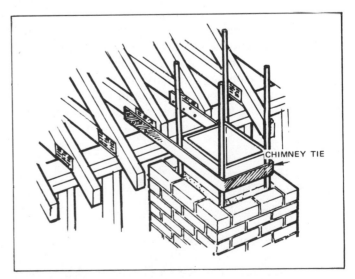

Anchor tie at roof line.

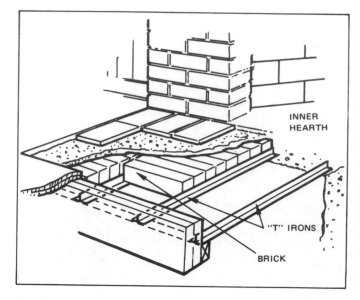

Simple hearth construction.

apply, they must be worked out in different ways.

Some hooded fireplaces, local codes permitting, can be built without a heavy foundation and masonry chimney. A fire brick hearth and firewall are built right over the flooring and the flue is provided by one or more patent chimneys. Since the computed opening of most hooded fireplaces is much greater than other types, the area of flue or flues must be proportionately greater.

Should you decide to build your own conventional masonry fireplace, you will learn much about laying brick and buying metal fireplace parts. The construction details and materials specifications in this chapter provide guidance in design and construction methods to enable you to carry out such a project. However, the authors recommend that you purchase a preformed heat-circulating fireplace and follow directions (see next chapter). Or, much easier, purchase a built-in pre-built, with its own factory-built chimney. This last is by far the best solution for the do-it-yourselfer. No foundation, little backache, and a lot of heat savings will be your rewards. This approach is particularly recommended for remodeling projects; otherwise, the damage potential to your living room (or other fireplace location), should you make a mistake in building your own conventional masonry fireplace, far exceeds the benefits you could conceivably gain.

Country club fireplace in large scale, with copper hood.

Relaxed dining is encouraged by handsome hooded fire.

Heat Circulating Fireplaces

More than three hundred years of experimentation have been devoted to the problem of going beyond the masonry fireplace and conserving heat ordinarily wasted up the chimney. The first step in this direction came about forty years ago with the introduction of the circulator fireplace.

Your masonry fireplace gives you only the radiated heat from the fire. A circulator fireplace gives you the radiated heat from the fire, plus the other kind—the circulated, convection heated air—greatly increasing the value received from the fuel you have paid for.

For the summer cottage, for the hunting cabin, or a between-season home heating system, or simply for use on those days when quick warmth will feel good but the use of the furnace is not quite justified, the circulator will pay for itself. In colder climates, the circulating fireplace will pay its small additional cost in reduction of fuel used by the main heating system. An additional advantage of this form of fireplace is its pre-built nature permitting ease of installation by the do-it-yourselfer or unskilled workman. This approach eliminates much of the measuring, checking, and guesswork involved in the construction of a conventional masonry fireplace. At the same time, the circulator retains the conventional appearance and charm.

Like a warm-air furnace, circulators have double-wall construction. The inner steel wall surrounds the fire chamber as does the fire brick in a masonry fireplace.

Between the inner and outer walls is an air chamber. Air comes into this chamber through grilles at floor level, is heated by contact with the walls of the fireplace, and discharged through registers to the interior of the home. Additional heating efficiency can be obtained by adding fans to the warm air ducts which also permits the heating of a greater area.

An example of the greater heat extraction from a circulator follows. A typical thirty-six-inch width of fireplace front opening has approximately one thousand square inches of area through which the heat radiates. A modern circulator of similar size will have nearly three thousand additional square inches of steel surface exposed either to the fire or the hot products of combustion. These steel surfaces heat the air passed over them by convection and pass it on to the room—or even adjacent rooms—through a system of strategically located intake and outlet ducts and grilles.

Circulating fireplaces can be located in any location that a conventional masonry fireplace may occupy.

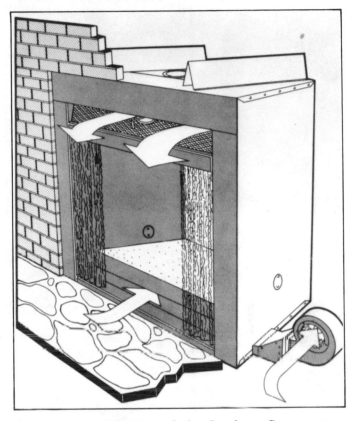

A new concept in heat-circulating fireplaces. Some are now completely pre-built, like this Western Fireplaces model. Air comes in at the bottom, circulates around refractory line, and then out the top. No masonry required except for hearth and decorative surround. Drawing courtesy of A. R. Wood

Their location on an interior wall may be dictated by the desire to heat two or more rooms from the several ducts available.

Circulators are available from some manufacturers as corner models, right and left hand and as through wall units opening on two rooms. In conventional fireplaces of this type, an extremely high percentage of the heat is lost up the chimney. With a circulator a good deal of this can be captured, and at the same time the unique charm of this type of fireplace is retained. Manufacturer's instructions about draft, flue size, chimney cap, etc., should be closely followed.

The placement of grilles often affects the appearance of circulators. In many cases, outlet grilles are located in the upper masonry of the fireplace front. Should some other location be preferred architecturally, projection of the fireplace from the plane of the wall leaves an inconspicuous side position available for

them. Shelving may further disguise their presence.

Ingenuity can often mask front-opening grilles. Latticed brickwork areas or stone baffles adorning the front at points of discharge have proven decorative and unobstrusive. Many other unique methods have been used, although the standard metal grilles are not necessarily offensive in appearance.

We should remember that the circulator is furnished by the manufacturer as a form for the masonry, not a supporting structure. The rules given elsewhere for footings, reinforcement, etc., of masonry fireplace construction still apply. The manufacturer's instructions furnished with the unit should be religiously followed.

Size and thickness of footing should be governed by local conditions and codes. Fire brick, with ash dump (if used), is laid in the hearth area. An extended hearth of at least eight inches on each side of the fireplace opening and with a minimum projection of sixteen inches must be provided. The hearth may be either raised or flush with the floor. A raised hearth may have provision for cold air intake under the hearth. In "tight" buildings provision should be made for com-

The all-metal heat circulating fireplace serves as an efficient fireplace with any desired exterior trim treatment. Air inlets or outlets that provide heat circulation can be extended to other rooms, as well as artistically treated in the finished trim. Photo courtesy of Majestic

This heat circulating fireplace unit was inserted into the fireplace of this older home. The unit exchanges heat on three sides of the firebox. Photo courtesy of Fuego

bustion air by a ventilating brick in the ash pit or other arrangement.

The fireplace unit is set in place on the hearth, and fastened to the hearth masonry. If required by the manufacturer, fiberglass or rock wool should cover the outside of the unit, and masonry should not contact the steel. Provide inlets and outlets as called for by instructions.

When masonry surround is complete, chimney should be built as described elsewhere in this book. Leave one-half inch or more space between metal and first flue tile.

In addition to the advantages of circulating fire-places previously mentioned, we may say:

- They take the guesswork out of fireplace building, affording a correctly formed interior.
- They save the expense of expert fireplacing brick-work.
- They insure a proper damper size and location.
- They provide a good smokeless fireplace, a cheerful fire, and heat that circulates to the far parts of the room.

Many of the advantageous features of heat circulating fireplaces have been incorporated into pre-built built-in fireplaces.

1—All the parts necessary for installing a pre-built fire-place.

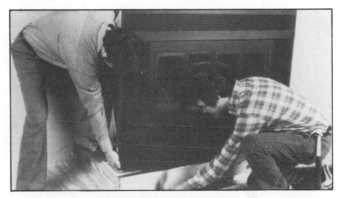

2—Position the unit on a plywood platform.

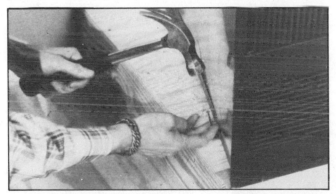

3—Secure the unit to the platform.

4—Attach vent assembly.

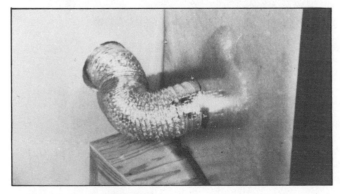

5—Finished vent assembly.

6—Frame in the pre-built unit.

7—Apply sheathing or plywood to frame.

8—Finish hearth as desired.

Corner model heat circulator with unique method of forming air inlets and outlets. Photo courtesy of Superior Fireplace Co.

Pre-Built Fireplaces

Esthetically, the traditional masonry fireplace, whether massive or petite, continues to be preferred over other types. However, the development of the Franklin stove and heat circulating fireplaces has been followed in recent years by the introduction of factory-built fireplaces requiring little of the high cost labor and hard-to-find skills required in masonry fireplacing.

Now it is possible to install a wood-burning fireplace without any concrete footings, without a masonry chimney and without relying on the fast-disappearing skills of masons whose hourly wages continue to climb out of proportion to the consumer's ability to pay.

Pre-built fireplaces are of two basic types: the conventional-appearing fireplace which is usually built into a wall (we call it a "built-in pre-built") and the metal fireplace, usually freestanding, which makes no pretence of looking traditional. Both types usually employ prefabricated flues although on occasion they can be vented into existing chimneys.

Pre-builts offer many advantages for installation by homeowners in existing or summer homes. The fact that no foundation is required permits the fireplace to be located anywhere the homeowner wishes. Upstairs or down, if you follow the manufacturer's installation instructions, you can be assured of a low cost, trouble-free fireplace. The completeness of the package makes buying a one stop operation with responsibility falling on only one supplier.

Built-in pre-built packaged fireplaces come complete from the factory to the builder's specifications. Damper, fire screen, hearth, hearth extension, surround, chimney, chimney housing and cap, together with easily understood instructons, may all be included.

Pre-builts have major national and regional code approvals. However, it is well to check with the local code involved before completing plans. "Zero clearance" approval of this type of fireplace means that most components may be installed directly on the subfloor and against wood framing. This is accomplished by insulation or by having multiple walls providing air spaces through which outside air circulates to keep outer surfaces safely cool.

These fireplaces are available as front opening models and as right- or left-hand corner models. Installation can be made projecting into the room, flush with the wall or with a raised hearth. Prefabricated flue may be angled around upper story fireplaces or other obstructions. In this manner, installations may be

With all the appearances of a conventional wood-burning fireplace, this all-metal prefabricated corner model wood-burning fireplace, complete with all-metal flue and simulated brick chimney top, can be easily installed in any home without special footings, foundation or masonry. Photo courtesy of Majestic

made in multiple housing with identical floor plans on successive floors.

As with conventional masonry fireplaces, the hearth, of incombustible material, should extend a minimum of sixteen inches from the front and eight inches on each side of the opening. Any of the conven-

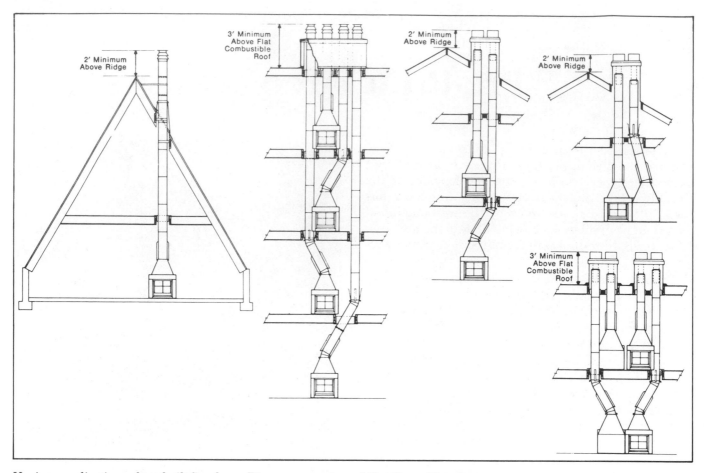

Various applications of pre-built fireplaces. Diagrams courtesy of Heatilator Fireplaces

tional materials may be used for the hearth, slate, brick, ceramic tile, terra cotta tile, etc. Installation of these materials can be made directly on the subfloor, usually without special support. Hearth extensions are optionally available from the manufacturer.

Surrounds may be any of the common materials, including brick. Of course, the rule about combustible materials, no closer than three and one-half inches to the side of the opening, must be followed. Mantels of combustible materials projecting over one and one-half inches must be at least twelve inches above the opening.

Manufacturers have a standard black glass surround available. Walls around the fireplace may be given the massive masonry feeling by applying well designed plastic stone or brick. Real brick and stone (one-half inch thick) is available in sheets which can be applied to the fireplace area. Mortar is tuck pointed in joints after application.

Metal fireplaces feature the greatest flexibility in location together with a minimum cost. They can vary from the simplest sheet metal firehood to expensive, factory-finished copper hoods with special-built masonry hearths. The metal hoods radiate heat on all sides and are thus more efficient as room heaters than

most masonry fireplaces.

To eliminate long remembered burns, some models are made with two and three wall thicknesses through which air circulates. These act like a furnace much as circulating fireplaces do. Clearance to combustible surfaces varies from zero to twenty-eight inches. Underwriters label or manufacturer's instructions should be checked on this point.

Freestanding, open on all sides, hoods have a tendency to smoke unless there is an adequate draft in the fireplace. The sudden opening of a window or door or even walking rapidly past can disturb the draft.

One solution is to pipe air from outside the house directly into or in front of the hearth or firepit. A fan placed at the top of the flue is another way to insure proper draft.

Since this type of hood has a rather large opening (360 degrees) the size of the flue should be ample. Also, some extra height to the flue will help insure the draft. To determine the area, measure the circumference of the hood and multiply by the distance from the firepit to the rim of the hood. The flue area should be at least one-eighth this size, and a metal disc damper should be provided.

The following are the requirements of the Universal

Free standing hood is center of attraction in this large room.
Photo courtesy of Goodwin

Building Code regarding hoods:

"Metal hoods used as part of a fireplace or barbecue shall be not less than No. 19 gauge copper, galvanized steel, or other equivalent corrosion-resistant ferrous metal with all seams and connections of smokeproof unsoldered constructions. The hood shall be sloped at an angle of 45° or less from the vertical and shall extend horizontally at least 6 inches beyond the limits of the firebox. Metal hoods shall be kept a minimum of 18 inches from combustible materials unless approved for reduced clearances."

Architects and homeowners are well advised to stick with standard, proprietary factory-built units of this type which are warranted to work by the manufacturer. For more expensive installations, some firms make custom-built units.

Standard metal fireplace units have the advantage of having been proved in many installations and usually bear the Underwriters label for further safety and local code acceptance. Most units are available with companion flue, housing, and chimney cap assemblies.

Although some metal wood-burning fireplaces can theoretically be placed on their legs over any type of floor, a hearth of concrete, brick, ceramic tile or other non-combustible material is recommended. Often a box containing sand, pebbles, or marble chips is used and can be as decorative as it is economical.

A firescreen is most desirable, as is the ash drawer provided with some units. The ash drawer will eliminate much of the after-fire cleanup.

Manufacturers of these units make them in many colors from the economical stove black to many bright porcelain colors. The colorful porcelain-on-steel is easy to keep clean.

Included in the group of standard metal fireplaces are several makes of the Franklin stoves and the traditional pot-bellied stove. Franklin stoves may be either free standing or placed in a masonry niche.

Metal fireplaces should be warmed up slowly because the rapid expansion of metal parts may cause warping of sheet metal or crazing of porcelain finish.

Metal fireplace designed for a corner installation. Brick provides fireproofing as well as decoration. Photo courtesy of Malm Fireplaces, Inc.

This conventional appearing wood-burning fireplace illustrates how the modern, all-metal prefabricated fireplace can be finished with any preference of exterior trim; as well as completely installed without masonry. Note woodbox on right. Photo courtesy of Majestic

*This metal pre-built fireplace was installed on a simple
brick hearth. Photo courtesy of Ember Box*

A uniquely different, but an unusually attractive version of a free standing wood-burner is found in this distinctive fireplace. In a choice of colors, the porcelain enamel finished fire chamber is accented by a matte black pedestal and base and vertical flue. Photo courtesy of Majestic

The straight line styling of this free standing wood-burning fireplace makes it especially versatile, both as to room location and room decor. Available for either top venting as shown or with rear outlet for mounting on the wall. Photo courtesy of Majestic

This pre-built unit was installed in the corner of this family room. The top vent goes through the ceiling, attic and roof. Photo courtesy of Ember Box

Electric and Gas Fireplaces

If you are an apartment dweller, yet a fireplace lover, if you cannot afford a fireplace in your new home, or should you abhor the chore of cleaning the hearth, keeping it supplied with wood and periodically cleaning the ashpit, you may find an answer in electric or gas fireplaces. They are available in a wide assortment of types and costs from a number of manufacturers.

Electric and gas fireplace equipment can be installed on existing masonry hearths, incorporated into most types of pre-built fireplaces, and some types you can even take with you when you move! The charm, beauty and warmth of a fireplace can be yours wherever you are.

Electric Fireplaces

Electric fireplaces are available in many types. The simplest do not provide heat, although they have log sets which flicker and glimmer like real logs. These use regular house current and can simply be plugged into a wall outlet. Others provide heat through electric heating elements, radiating heat into the room much as wood logs.

Electric log sets for installation in existing fireplaces are also available. You can have them with or without heating elements.

The ultimate electric fireplace provides forced air heat in response to a thermostat installed on a wall on the opposite side of the room. These sometimes require three-wire outlets much like an electric range. Heat output on some models is as much as 6000 BTUs, enough to heat one or more rooms.

Electric models are available which can be moved about like a piece of furniture. These are complete with wood mantel, simulated brick hearth and facing, and may even include a complete set of fireplace furnishings. The decor of the room is not fixed; the fireplace can be moved from wall to wall, room to room, and you can even take it along when you move.

Safety is a feature in electric fireplaces. You need only be sure that the outlet you plug into has adequate amperage and that the unit you buy carries an Underwriters label.

Gas Fireplaces

The same advantages of lowered cost, beauty, and simplicity of installation are typical of the modern gas fireplace. Their variety ranges from complete room-heating units to gas log sets for already existing fire-

Wall hung electric fireplace. Photo courtesy of Fasco

places where wood is unavailable or too expensive.

The factory-built gas-fired fireplace saves on construction costs because no masonry or brick foundations are required. Installation requires no special tools or craftsmen in many cases. Pre-assembled units fit in place on the existing floor and a carpenter merely has to frame the unit in. Finish trim can be selected to match the decor of the room, or units complete with finish trim or with panels are available.

These units are manufactured for both natural and L.P. gas. The only precaution the buyer should take is to purchase only units which meet the standards of the

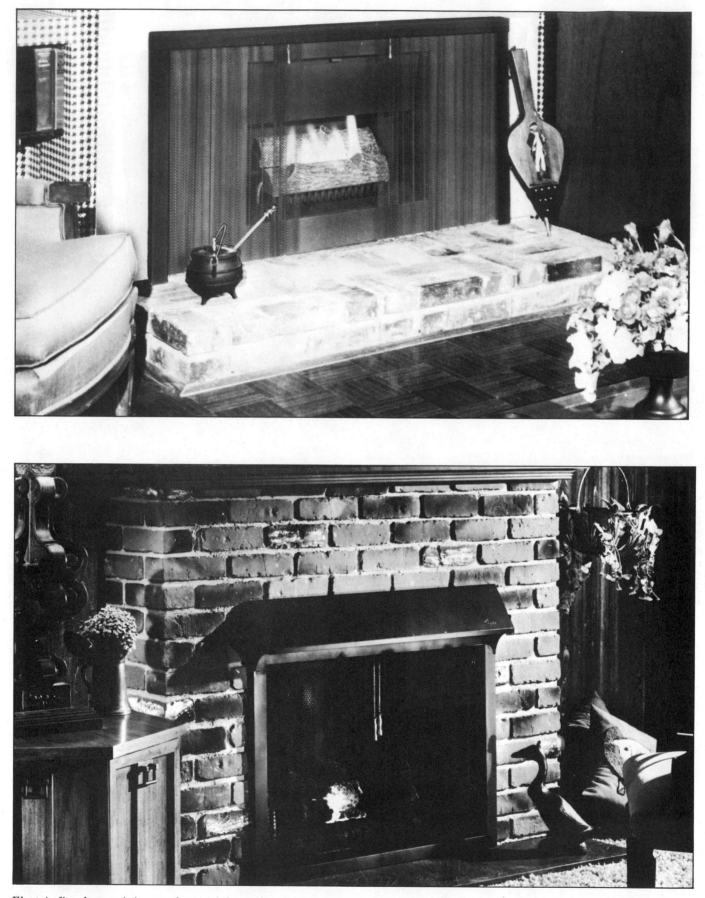

Electric fireplace unit is complete with hearth and mantel that can be moved like furniture. Photo courtesy of Fasco

Showing how a compact gas-fired fireplace by means of a choice of available screen assemblies, can be given the illusion of a large size, realistic wood-burning fireplace when used in larger rooms. Lighted by push-button and vented with prefabricated metal flue. Photo courtesy of Majestic.

American Gas Association. It is also wise to check local building code specifications.

One popular compact unit is no deeper than a bookcase and thus can fit in a small apartment or mobile home. At the other extreme, there are models which contain both a gas fireplace and a self-contained thermostatically controlled heating unit which can be used separately or together to heat completely a large room.

Safety pilots, pushbutton controls for instant firing, blowers to circulate heat throughout rooms, all are offered the homeowner interested in gas fireplaces. Many pilots are self-generating and do not have to connect into a house or building electrical system.

Units are prepared for ½-inch or ⅜-inch gas plumbing through the floor, side, or back to the gas control valve. They can be vented with standard type B gas vent or into an existing approved flue. The gas vent is much more economical than those provided for solid fuel pre-builts.

Gas fireplaces can be used in multiple housing. In high-rise buildings the required flues fit easily between studs into a normal four-inch wall with only the usual elementary sheetmetal duct work. Where a flue is not already available, factory-made prefabricated vent packages can be supplied with the fireplace.

Homeowners with existing fireplaces who are interested in switching to gas log sets will find these vastly changed from the early models which frequently were justly characterized as "artificial" looking. Modern manufacturers offer an infinite variety of log sets simulating various woods and giving a realistic, cheery flame. These woods range from the more conventional white birch and oak through twisted cypress

Electric fireplace with wood mantel and screen. Photo courtesy of Readybuilt

to the more exotic effect of simulated tiki and manzanita log sets.

It must be stressed that gas log sets, if not part of a factory-manufactured complete fireplace unit, should be operated only in a vented fireplace with a chimney free of any obstructions and with the damper fully open.

Energy Efficient Fireplaces

A properly built conventional masonry fireplace contributes much cheer but little heat to the home. Experts agree that only about 10 percent of the potential heat goes into the room; the rest goes up the chimney. A poorly built or carelessly operated fireplace can cause a net loss in heat. In this chapter, we will present some ways you can change that—for old and new homes alike.

All Homes

Damper Keep the damper tightly closed when the fireplace is not in use.

Glass Doors These may be closed when the family retires, leaving open only the slots at the bottom to provide air so the fire can burn itself out. Otherwise, a great deal of heat will be lost up the chimney once the fire has burned itself out and before anyone gets up to close the damper. Glass doors, especially, waste heat when left closed with an active fire. Nearly all the heat goes up the chimney!

Chimolator This device closes off the top of the flue when there is no fire. The chimolator keeps the flue warm, which helps start the fire and minimizes creosote deposits.

Tubular Grates A recent development, C-shaped metal tubes functioning as a grate are excellent heat savers. Cold room air comes in the bottom, is heated and expelled out the top into the room. Many models come equipped with a blower. This low-cost item is an excellent heat-saving investment for any fireplace.

Heat Exchangers Placed between the stove or fireplace and the flue, they function by extracting additional heat from the hot gases going up the flue. Heat exchangers are most effective on the less-efficient stoves, such as an open front Franklin or the metal pre-built fireplaces. Some models come equipped with a blower.

Insulation and Weatherstripping For both new and old homes there will soon be higher insulation thicknesses, storm windows and weatherstripping mandated by federal energy standards in order to conserve energy, whether it comes from your fireplace or your regular furnace. Remember that a tight house will require air for fireplace combustion. Provision should be made for this at or near the fireplace. Some pre-built fireplaces come with this feature already built in.

New Homes

Location A fireplace located on the outside wall is a cause of much heat loss, even when the fireplace is not operating. Heat loss through the surrounding masonry walls is much greater than through surrounding insulated walls.

There are two solutions. First, locate the fireplace and its chimney entirely within the heated portions of the home. Thus, heat loss will be minimized and, when in use, the heat from the fireplace and the chimney will radiate into the home. If you insist on locating the fireplace on an outside wall, and you may have valid

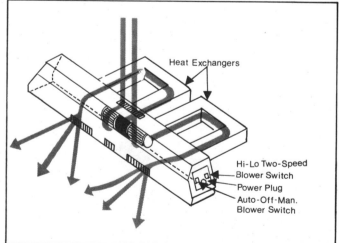

Twin blowers circulate air over the fire, expelling warmed air into the room. May be installed for new or old fireplace. Art courtesy of Duo Therm

This unit is one of the most energy efficient fireplace inserts available. Notice the large heat exchange vents. Photo courtesy of Martin Industries

planning and aesthetic reasons for this, insulate the wall by building the fireplace within the insulated outside wall of the home. Or, build an insulated brick wall outside the fireplace/chimney wall.

Damper Be sure to install a tightly closing, adjustable damper. This will aid you in controlling the draft, and the amount of heat going up the chimney, and prevent a smoky fire.

Heat Circulating Fireplace With the use of one of these factory-built metal inserts you recirculate much of the heat now going up the fireplace chimney.

Pre-built Fireplaces Many of these have heat circulating features, and because the dimensions are all predetermined, you need not depend on unskilled workmen for the proper dimensions. Some pre-built fireplaces approach the wood stove in efficiency.

Electric and Gas Fireplaces Since the electric fireplace does not have a flue, it avoids much of the cost and heat loss common to other fireplaces. Some gas fireplaces have features that permit the heat to be used in the room similar to a space heater.

Wood Stove We could say: Don't put in a fireplace at all; this would probably save the most energy with reference to your present heating equipment. But a wood stove such as the Jotul Combi or the Franklin stove with opening front doors could best answer both needs—cheery open fire like a conventional fireplace, or an efficient wood-burning stove for supplemental or emergency heat. If you like, go all the way; install several stoves and forget about gas or oil bills.

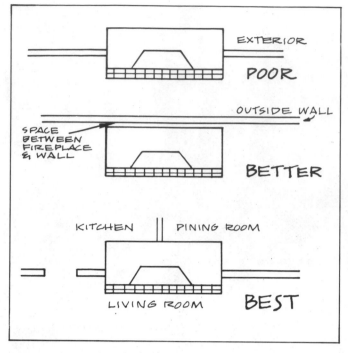

Location of fireplace greatly affects heat loss.

Existing Homes

There is little you can do about the location of an existing fireplace. It is probably too costly to move. But if it is on the outside wall, you can insulate it as shown above.

Construction Check to see if your chimney or fireplace is troubled with any of the faults described in the last chapter. Correcting these may not only save energy, but your home as well!

Wood Stove You may find it advantageous to brick up or cover the fireplace opening and install a thimble for a wood stove connector, thus using the fireplace flue for a stove. But don't use it for both!

Heat exchanger is installed here on a parlor stove. Maximum heat is extracted from flue gases with the aid of blower. Can be installed on stoves, freestanding fireplaces, or furnaces. This parlor stove has removable nickeled top to permit cooking. Fan can be used for summer cooling. Photo courtesy of Calcinator

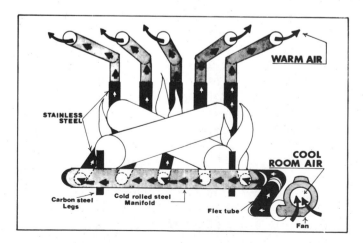

The fireplace heating grate is a one-piece unit that combines a conventional grate for logs and an air intake/blower system for circulating warmed air. After a 40 minute preheat period, the intake may be turned on. It draws in cool air that is then warmed in the pipes and blown into the room. Nozzles swivel, so heated air can be directed where needed. Art courtesy of New England Fireplace Heaters Inc.

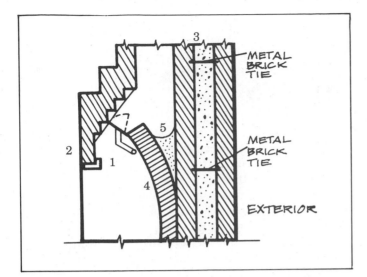

How to insulate a fireplace and chimney that project to the outside. 1, Damper, 2. Facing, 3. Mineral Insulation, 4. Firebrick Lining, 5. Cement Fillet.

This two-speed blower draws cool air into the fireplace where it is warmed and then forced back into the room. Photo courtesy of Sears

This fireplace insert features a thermostatically controlled blower. Photo courtesy of Suburban

The above blower installed on a regular fireplace. The blower increases energy efficiency. Photo courtesy of Sears

This insert features a built-in humidifier and removable ash pan. Photo courtesy of Suburban

Wood Stoves

To many, the most attractive feature of wood heat is the notion of independence, of self-sufficiency. No need to be concerned about what bureaucracies or utilities—governmental or corporate—are going to do to you. Your fuel supply is under your control. As the price of heat from oil, gas, electricity or propane increases, as it inevitably will, you can be secure in the knowledge that your family is safe from freezing and from rationing. And the feeling of security is magnified when you save hundreds of dollars every year.

Beyond security, there are other psychological benefits of wood heat. As in an earlier time, it can unite family members and activities. While Dad cuts and

The "Cannonball" pot bellied stove. Manufactured since 1902, this model has a nickeled waistband and foot warming rails. Photo courtesy of Pioneer Lamps and Stoves

splits wood, the children stack and carry it in. Better than being glued to the TV all day! With modern central heating, the family disperses to various rooms, becoming less of a family and more a group of people living in the same house. In a wood-heated home, each member of the family finds a place close to the fire, reading, doing homework, knitting, discussing or simply watching the fire.

Efficiency

Whatever your reason for going to wood heat, you will find that a conventional fireplace, even with heat circulating features, is the least efficient method of converting wood to heat. Most of the heat goes up the flue. But with a well designed, properly installed stove, it is possible to achieve efficiencies of over 50 percent of the potential heat. Some manufacturers advertise as much as 70 percent, but this is doubtful under other than laboratory conditions.

Wood-heat efficiency is difficult to achieve because the efficient stove must function as a gas burner, burning the gases distilled from the wood. This accounts for 40 percent of the heat potential. At the same time, a stove must function as a charcoal burner for the balance of the heat potential. All this is further complicated by the irregular shape of the fuel. It is a credit to the skill of modern stove manufacturers, both U.S. and foreign, that they have been able to develop such efficient products.

Selection

Luckily, wood stoves have not become standardized, as have many products in today's industrialized age. Stoves come in all sizes, from little foot warmers to giants that burn four-foot logs. There are styles available that allow you to see the fire, or to close it up tightly for maximum efficiency. And some can be used either way. Others are made to burn *either* wood or oil. Thermostatically controlled draft is standard on many of the quality products. Colors are available, as are a wide choice of materials, including steel, cast iron, tile, brick, etc. And you can cook on top, or inside, of some models.

Stoves are of two basic types, radiant or circulating. The radiant stoves are those that you are most familiar with. The fire inside heats the outer skin of steel or cast iron, which radiates heat throughout the room.

This unique wood stove is a far cry from the pot bellied stoves that warmed America's first homes. The vent passes through the wall rather than the ceiling. This feature per- *mits the fireplace to be installed adjacent to any outside wall. Photo courtesy of Schrader Stoves*

People feel comfortable in an area heated to a relatively low temperature by radiant heat, if the area is protected from drafts. Radiant stoves are the closest thing to fireplaces without the energy waste. Despite parents' repeated cautions, babies and children can be severely burned by one touch. Dresses and trousers can be scorched when the wearer gets a little too close.

Circulating stoves have the firebox surrounded by a cabinet through which air circulates, is warmed, and returned to the room, often assisted by an electric blower. The temperature of the cabinet is warm but seldom warm enough to burn. Usually thermostatically controlled, you seldom see the fire. Circulating stoves are about as far away from the fireplace—with its cheer and dangers—as you can get.

Location and Number of Stoves Required

Frequently, this is decided by the location of an existing chimney. But modern, safe, prefabricated flues permit you to locate stoves anywhere in the home at little additional cost.

Well-insulated, draft-free modern homes may be heated by only one stove, with an extra one for extreme cold spells. Of course, a blower-equipped circulator will tend to move the heat about the home more effectively than a radiant stove.

The first stove usually will be located in the living room, close to the kitchen. But the kitchen may be heated by a wood-burning range. A stove might be

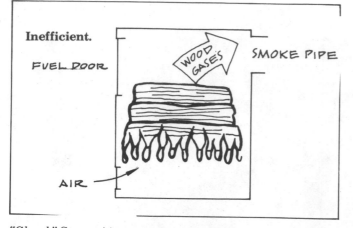

Inefficient.

"Chunk" Stove—Air enters through ash door. Large volume of wood gases escape out smoke pipe.

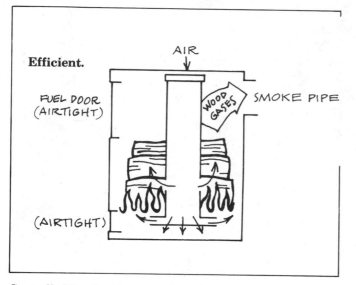

Efficient.

Controlled Draft—Air enters above, is preheated and spread across and above the fire. Some wood gases escape.

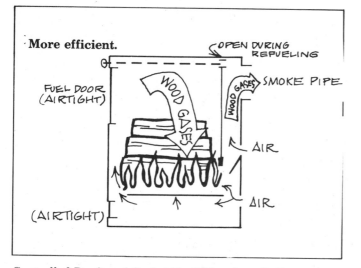

More efficient.

Controlled Draft and Sealed Fuel Chamber—Pull of draft and small self-generated pressure of wood gases in sealed fuel chamber force them into fire. Small amounts escape.

Three drawings showing different levels of efficiency in burning the wood gases in stoves which account for 40 percent of the heat potential in wood.

provided in the bedroom area. The location of a living room stove close to the stairway going upstairs may warm the upstairs, provided the BTU output is high enough. Another way is to cut an old-fashioned grill into the second floor, over the downstairs stove, allowing some heat to move through it to upstairs bedrooms. Avoid the mistake of thinking that such heat access to the second floor is going to heat it as warm as the room below. There is a limit on the heat output of all stoves, and you may need another stove on the second floor to keep it as warm as you would like.

For occasional use, stoves may be needed in the basement, laundry area, workshop or garage. These may be small, inexpensive sheet metal stoves. Remember that the safety requirements are just as important for stoves that see only occasional use as they are for stoves used every day.

Safety When the energy crisis hit in 1974, panic-inspired carelessness in the installation of wood or coal stoves caused many fires with the attendant loss of life and injuries. For details on safety rules, and case histories where they have been violated, read the National Fire Protection Association's booklet on Safety.

Buying a Stove Don't buy a used stove without it being checked by an expert. Remember, real antique stoves were heavily used in their day and their remaining useful life may be short.

A new stove should be sturdily built, preferably of cast iron, and purchased from a reliable dealer that has experts on his staff. The Scandinavian stoves are generally of the highest quality, but some U.S. stoves now equal or exceed them, at a lower cost. If there is a possibility that you may burn coal in the stove, be sure that the stove can handle it.

Flues and Chimney Connectors (Stove Pipe) Existing masonry flues should be inspected for potential difficulties. Factory-built chimneys should be tested and approved by nationally recognized laboratories such as Underwriters Laboratories, Inc. (UL). They should be installed only with the required clearances from combustible materials, as specified by the manufacturer. Chimneys should protrude above the roof as shown.

Should you wish to use an existing fireplace flue for a stove, it is best to close the opening with brick or with a sheet metal cover. The connector for the stove may then be run into a thimble in the closure. If the stove is too high for this, then cut a hole into the flue itself above the smoke chamber, installing a thimble. Don't try to use the flue for both a fireplace and a stove. Just consider the open-front stove as your fireplace when used in this fashion.

Room heater is a circulator in a woodtone cabinet. Cast iron fire box, with flues to direct oxygen to top of the fire for efficient burning of wood gases. Interchangeable grates for wood or coal. Automatic draft control for wood or coal. Photo courtesy of Monarch

This front loading stove provides a romantic view of the flames through the tempered glass window. Exterior is red porcelain enamel with matching stovepipes. Photo courtesy of Monarch

Old-timers will tell you about running several stoves into one flue. Don't. With modern low-cost factory-built chimneys, there is little reason why you should take this risk. NFPA, in their booklet, recommends against it. But should you wish to live dangerously, the NFPA provides a table of square inches of flue capacity related to combined BTU input of the stoves and height of the flue.

In masonry chimneys it is preferable to use a thimble. It should be installed so as not to protrude into the flue with high temperature cement. The connector (stove pipe) then may be inserted into the thimble (see drawing on page 80).

Where a connector passes through a partition, it must be located and sized to meet the following conditions, according to the NFPA:

1. If a ventilated-type metal thimble—as shown on page 80—is used, the thimble must be at least 12 inches larger in diameter than the chimney connector.

2. Where a metal or burned fire-clay thimble is used, the thimble must be surrounded on all sides by not less than eight inches of brickwork or equivalent fireproofing material.

3. Combustible material must be cut out of the partition wall for a sufficient distance to provide not less than 18 inches clearance on all sides of the connector. Any material used to close the opening must be of non-combustible material.

Connectors are required by NFPA to have a pitch of ¼ inch to the linear foot, so that the elevation at the chimney is higher than at the stove. The connector should have no sharp turns, as few sweeping bends as possible, and be securely supported. Joints should be tight.

This refreshingly different French imported Petit Goding wood/coal stove is available in two sizes and four colors. Photo courtesy of Bow & Arrow Stove Co.

This stove can also be used for cooking. Photo courtesy of Pine Barren

Jotul Combi #4 with door closed for maximum heating efficiency. With door slid under unit, it provides the cheer of a fireplace. Photo courtesy of Kristia Associates

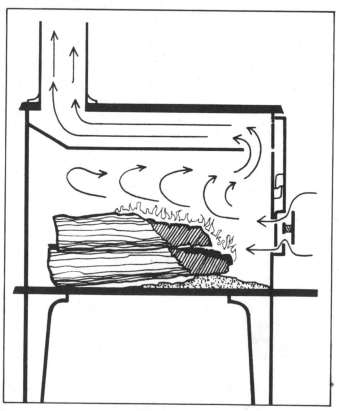

An easy way to install a new stove is to use your old fireplace flue. The entrance of the fireplace can be blocked off; then either use the old flue or install new piping up through the chimney. Drawing courtesy of Dept. of Agriculture

Typical smoke flow pattern and baffle system in Scandinavian stoves. Note how wood burns from one end, like a cigaret. Drawing courtesy of Southport Stores

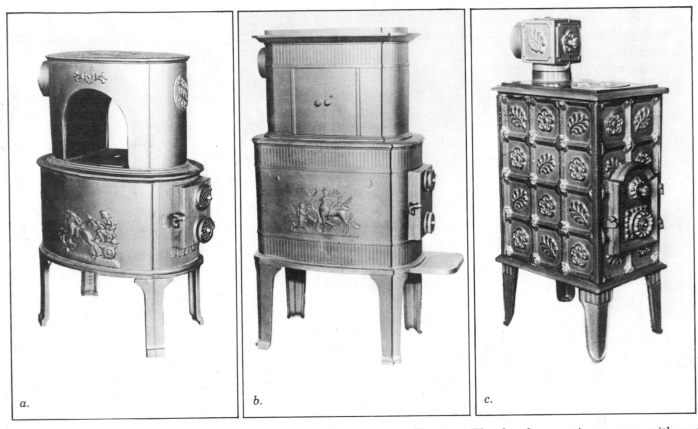

Several Lange stoves from Denmark. Photo courtesy of Scandinavian Stoves, Inc.

   a. Model 6303, with added heat chamber on top to get more heat out of the same amount of wood.

   b. Model 6302K. Second heating chamber added to a smaller stove. The chamber contains an oven, with vent for temperature regulation and cooking plates. Will heat a large area, and handle cooking and baking at the same time.

   c. A parlor stove patterned after the European tile stoves.

It is important that an automatic draft regulator or a manually operated damper be installed in the connector, either horizontally or vertically. This is best installed near the stove for convenience of operation.

Stove Clearances Standard heating stoves should have clearances from combustible materials of 36 inches from top, front, back and sides. Circulators and some specially built stoves have been laboratory approved for lesser clearances. Be guided by these if the manufacturer clearly states the approved clearances in writing. A salesman's assurances are valueless.

Under the stove, 18 inches of clearance should be provided from combustible floors. This may be reduced to four inches if the area under the stove is completely covered with at least 24-gauge sheet metal or other non-combustible material. The metal should extend out 18 inches on the side where ashes are removed.

Should you wish to install a radiant stove closer to a standard 2 × 4 wall with plaster or drywall, you may apply brick, asbestos board or tile on the wall. A layer of aluminum foil under these materials will help reflect the heat. But even here, do not reduce the clearance under 18 inches. Don't forget that radiant heat can go through brick or other non-combustibles to ignite the wood underneath.

Creosote Creosote deposits in the flue or the connector are problems that go along with wood stoves. It is caused by improperly burned wood gases that condense in the connector or flue and later are ignited by an extremely hot fire. Once creosote is ignited it burns with an extremely hot fire that may damage mortar joints or ignite nearby combustible materials.

The creosote formation can be minimized by providing air to the upper portion of the fire to insure combustion of the gases. A cool, smoldering fire will often result from reducing the draft overnight, and cause poor combustion of the gases. The air-tight stoves, such as the European models, are said to be a problem in this regard. For this reason, we recommend a short connector between the stove and the flue with air-tight stoves. Creosote buildups are minimized with factory-built chimneys because they warm up rapidly, minimizing condensation.

Creosote buildup can be reduced by having a high fire at least part of the day, with the stove open, if it is that type. Otherwise, keep the connectors and the flue clean. Disassemble the connector and clean periodically. Scrape the flue by running some old tire chains up and down from the top.

The use of wood stoves for heating, even occasionally, requires much more vigilance from the homeowner and his family than do central oil and gas furnaces. Understanding and following the foregoing suggestions will help keep you safe. One final suggestion—mount a fire extinguisher near the stove. Be careful, and enjoy!

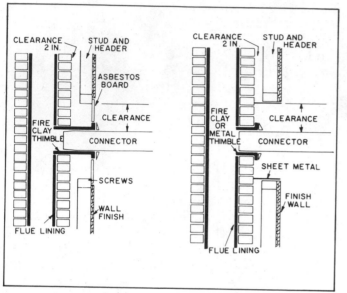

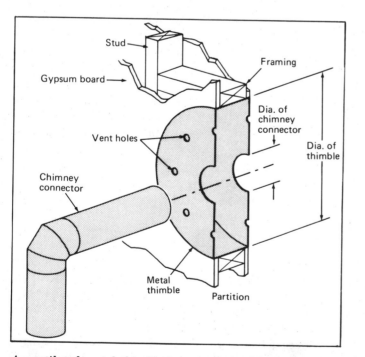

Two methods of connecting a chimney connector to a chimney flue where the connector must pass through a combustible partition wall. Instead of the asbestos board shown, sheet metal may be used, or a metal lath and plaster finish may be applied at that area.

A ventilated metal thimble is one permissible method of installing a chimney connector through a combustible partition wall.

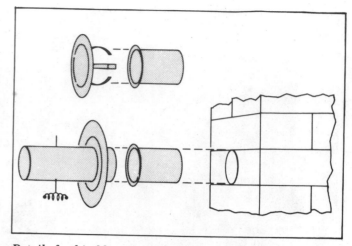

Detail of a thimble with a blank cover being removed, and a chimney connector being installed. The chimney connector shows a damper.

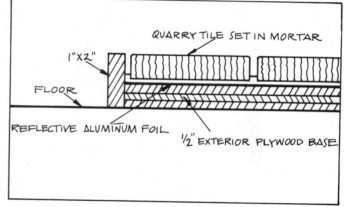

A quarry tile base you can make for your hearth or stove. Stove should be at least 4 inches from base.

Wood as Fuel

Wood is the only fuel resource that is constantly being renewed. Trees not only convert solar energy, but store it in the form of wood, for future use.

The convenient fossil fuels like coal, oil and gas exist in the earth in fixed amounts. New discoveries do not increase the real reserves of these fuels. Starting a century ago, the use of the convenience fuels replaced wood as a fuel in the industrialized world. Now the energy crisis has caused a revival in the use of fuel wood.

Wood is a clean fuel, when burned completely and efficiently. The products of its combustion are similar to those which result from natural decay in the forest. If we utilized the wood wasted in our forests and in industry, we could heat at least half and probably all of the homes in the United States, without depleting our forests.

It is not true, as people believe, that most wood goes into construction. Worldwide, in 1967, 43 percent of the wood cut was used for fuel and only 34 percent for construction. The fuel-wood percentage varies greatly in various parts of the world. Latin American countries used wood for 83 percent of their needs; Africa, 89 percent; Mainland China, 77 percent; Western Europe, 20 percent; and in the United States, only six percent.

Despite the availability and low cost of wood fuel, not everyone will heat their homes and cook their food with wood. The logistics of moving huge quantities of wood to a metropolis present insuperable problems. But we might seriously consider the creation of urban forests and backyard woodlots to produce fuel at the point of use. A welcome by-product of this policy would be to improve air quality through absorption of carbon dioxide and the creation of oxygen. The potential for this type of fuel wood production improves every year as new, faster-growing trees are developed by forest researchers.

The use of wood as a fuel has expanded rapidly in the few years since the oil embargo. The greatest growth has been in rural areas and in small towns, which are close to the fuel resources. Interest is now so great that there is a magazine for wood fuel users, called the *Wood Burning Quarterly*.

During the worst of the oil shortage, it was nearly impossible to purchase wood-burning stoves. Now, private enterprise has created efficient wood-burning devices from hot-water heaters to central heating furnaces. And new products are being introduced daily.

How it Burns

One pound of properly air-dried fuel wood will contain about 20 percent moisture and can generate 5800 BTU's (British Thermal Units). In heat content, it takes about one and one-half pounds of wood to equal one pound of coal or 22 pounds of wood to equal a gallon of fuel oil. Fourteen pounds of wood equal 100 cubic feet of gas.

Before wood burns, the moisture content must first be driven off in the form of steam. Next, the volatile wood gases are distilled from the wood. These include

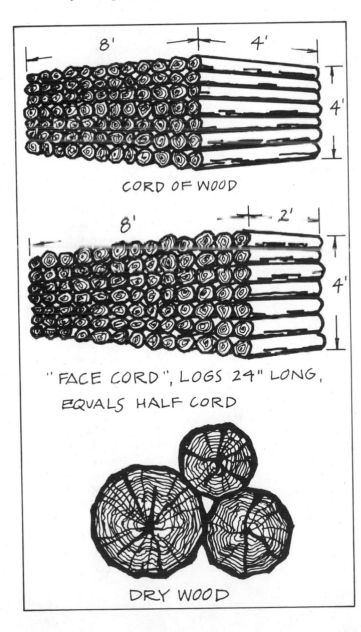

CORD OF WOOD

"FACE CORD", LOGS 24" LONG, EQUALS HALF CORD

DRY WOOD

methanol or wood alcohol. About 40 percent of the heat from wood can be from the combustion of these gases. "Can be" because, unless oxygen and a firebox temperature of about 1000°F are provided at the right place, these gases will go up the flue, to condense and cause creosote problems. The rest of the wood is burned as charcoal.

The table shows the relative heating value, per cord, of various woods compared with coal. From the table, it appears that Shagbark Hickory may be the best buy, with its 24.6 million BTU's per cord. But there are other considerations. Price, as always, is a dominant one. So is availability. Splitability is another. Another way to classify fuel wood is shown in the table.

Approximate Weight and Heating Value per Cord (80 Actual Cu. Ft.) of Different Woods, Green and Air-Dry (20 Percent Moisture)

Woods	Weight, lb.		Available heat, million BTU		Equivalent in coal tons	
	Green	Air-dry	Green	Air-dry	Green	Air-dry
Ash	3,840	3,440	16.5	20.0	0.75	0.91
Aspen	3,440	2,160	10.3	12.5	0.47	0.57
Beech, American	4,320	3,760	17.3	21.8	0.79	0.99
Birch, yellow	4,560	3,680	17.3	21.3	0.79	0.97
Douglas-fir	3,200	2,400	13.0	18.0	0.59	0.82
Elm, American	4,320	2,900	14.3	17.2	0.65	0.78
Hickory, shagbark	5,040	4,240	20.7	24.6	0.94	1.12
Maple, red	4,000	3,200	15.0	18.6	0.68	0.85
Maple, sugar	4,480	3,680	18.4	21.3	0.84	0.97
Oak, red	5,120	3,680	17.9	21.3	0.81	0.97
Oak, white	5,040	3,920	19.2	22.7	0.87	1.04
Pine, eastern white	2,880	2,080	12.1	13.3	0.55	0.60
Pine, southern yellow	4,000	2,600	14.2	20.5	0.64	0.93

Ratings for Firewood

HARDWOOD TREES	Relative amount of heat	Easy to burn	Easy to split	Does it have heavy smoke?	Does it pop or throw sparks?	General rating and remarks
Ash, red oak, white oak, beech, birch, hickory, hard maple, pecan, dogwood	High	Yes	No	No	No	Excellent
Soft maple, cherry, walnut	Medium	Yes	Yes	No	No	Good
Elm, sycamore, gum	Medium	Medium	No	Medium	No	Fair—contains too much water when green
Aspen, basswood, cottonwood, yellow-poplar	Low	Yes	Yes	Medium	No	Fair—but good for kindling
SOFTWOOD TREES						
Southern yellow pine, Douglas-fir	High	Yes	Yes	Yes	No	Good but smoky
Cypress, redwood	Medium	Medium	Yes	Medium	No	Fair
White cedar, western red cedar, eastern red cedar	Medium	Yes	Yes	Medium	Yes	Good—excellent for kindling
Eastern white pine, western white pine, sugar pine, ponderosa pine, true firs	Low	Medium	Yes	Medium	No	Fair—good kindling
Tamarack, larch	Medium	Yes	Yes	Medium	Yes	Fair
Spruce	Low	Yes	Yes	Medium	Yes	Poor—but good for kindling.

Source: U.S. Dept. of Agriculture—Forest Service
The table above shows the relative ratings of a variety of dried woods.

Soft woods such as pine, spruce and fir are easy to ignite because they are resinous. They burn rapidly with a hot flame. However, since a fire built entirely of softwoods burns out quickly, it requires frequent attention and replenishment. This can be a boon if you want a quick-warming fire or a short fire that will burn out before you go to bed.

For a long-lasting fire, use the heavier hardwoods such as beech, birch, maple and oak. These species burn less vigorously than soft woods and with a shorter flame. Since woods are of different compositions, they ignite at different temperatures and give off different heat values; therefore it is beneficial to mix light and heavy woods to achieve the ideal fire.

Aroma is best derived from the woods of fruit trees, such as apple and cherry, and nut trees such as beech, hickory and pecan. Their smoke generally resembles the fragrance of the tree's fruit. Wood from fruit and nut trees often sells for more per cord than wood with greater heating values. But sometimes an agreement with an orchard owner to keep his dead wood cleaned up will result in free wood from this source.

How Much Wood?

Do you have only an occasional fire in your fireplace to drive off a fall chill? Or do you build the occasional fire to soothe the troubled soul?

Do you want to use one or more stoves for supplemental or standby heat in case your regular fuel source fails? Or are you going to go all out and heat your home, your hot water, and cook your meals with wood? Your objective will dictate the amount of fuel wood you must acquire.

The average home in northern climates can be heated, including hot water and cooking, with six cords a year. But a well-insulated, modern home with well-sealed windows and doors can be heated with as little as two cords per year. At the other end of the scale, the drafty old farmhouse may require twenty cords per year.

Wood is sold by the cord, or a stack of logs, round or split, four feet by four feet by eight feet.

This cord is 128 cubic feet, with weight varying with the density of the wood. Due to the irregular shape of logs, the average cord of wood actually contains only 80 cubic feet of wood.

Since few people burn logs either four or eight feet in length, wood-sellers sell a "face cord"—that is, a four by eight foot face, cut to the usable length. A face cord of 24-inch pieces is actually a half a cord, and of 16-inch pieces is one-third of a cord. Inexperienced wood buyers sometimes pay for a full cord but actually receive a face cord or some other "cord" invented by the wood seller.

In some parts of the country, firewood is sold by the ton. A ton of air-dry, dense hardwood (best-burning oak, hickory, maple) equals about one-half a cord. When buying by weight, look for dry wood of the more dense species. Don't pay for extra water, which with green wood can amount to half your purchase. You can tell dryness by radial cracks in the ends of the pieces or by striking one piece against the other. Wet wood will give a "thunk" when struck.

Sources

In the 20s, when I was growing up in Detroit, our home was heated by a coal furnace. The dry, hardwood cuttings we used to kindle the furnace and for our fireplace came from local auto plants which used it for car bodies and car prototypes. Not only did it burn well, but the curves and shapes made excellent building blocks for imaginative children. Wood is no longer used to build car bodies, but it is used in many other industries.

Where I work, coils of steel are received on heavy pallets of oak and maple. Unless damaged, these pallets are returned to the steel company for re-use. I haul home the damaged pieces of 3 × 4, 4 × 6, etc. This is more than enough for my modest wood-burning needs.

You may not have access to car-body scrap or pallets, but in every part of the country wood is used for many purposes and the resulting scrap is often available for the asking.

Much wood is available in dumps or landfills. As much as 30 percent of the debris in some town dumps consists of burnable wood, including the logs, limbs and tops of trees toppled by storms.

Logs of elm trees killed by Dutch Elm disease can be burned as firewood. These should be used the first winter or before the spring following the tree's death. This prevents the disease-carrying beetles from emerging and infecting healthy elms. If you can't burn all the dead elm wood before spring, remove and burn the bark so that larvae and eggs are destroyed.

Fuel wood may be available from your state and national forests. Harvesting of saw logs or cutting to improve wildlife habitat annually leaves millions of cords on the ground to rot. Contact your district office for acquisition permission and directions.

Artificial Logs

Individually wrapped logs sold by supermarkets and other mass merchandisers are usually made of compressed sawdust and other wood by-products. They are treated with paraffin to insure lighting and burning. Some are treated to emit colored flames and incense.

These logs should not be burned in stoves of any kind, in barbecues, or used for cooking. They should be burned one at a time and not broken up or added to an existing fire. They can be used to help get real logs started, but this is expensive kindling. Do not use tongs or a poker with these logs. In sum, these logs will provide a small measure of fireplace cheer if real wood is not available, or if you don't want to go to the trouble of building a real fire. But, again, exercise caution.

Neither the compressed sawdust logs nor the home-made rolled up newspaper logs can give the heat or the ambiance of oak, maple or cherry logs. You need not buy a machine to make newspaper logs. You simply put newspaper sections to soak overnight in your bath-tub with a little detergent. In the morning, roll up the paper around a broom handle, remove the handle and let them stand on end for several weeks.

Sorry to be so negative, but another note of caution: In investigating the unknown cause of lead poisoning in a baby, pediatricians of the State University of New York at Syracuse determined that the poisoning occur-red as the result of burning papers with colored ink (containing lead) in the fireplace. The child had absorbed the lead either by breathing the smoke or licking fingers soiled with fireplace dust. The doctors urge parents not to burn newspapers, magazines and other papers printed with colored ink anywhere in the home, and to make sure the room is well-ventilated if they burn papers printed with black ink. Why not just take the papers to your local recycling center?

Grow Your Own

A few fast-growing trees in your own backyard can furnish enough wood for occasional fireplace use. A one-acre woodlot will yield one cord per year, without overcutting.

A 40-acre woodlot cannot only provide home heating but an income from the sale of sawings, pulpwood and fuel wood. The tables show that the best fuels are the slow-growing hardwoods. But consider modern forest management practices of planting fast-growing spe-cies, like newly developed strains of quaking aspen or other hardwoods.

Despite aspen's low fuel value, it more than makes up for it in rapidity of growth. One newly developed strain grows six feet in the first year! Check with your state foresters for their recommendation.

Hardwoods such as aspen benefit wildlife. Conifers produce what we call a "green desert" with little wild-life. The aspen forest or ecosystem, when harvested properly, provides ideal habitat for deer, ruffed grouse, woodcock, rabbit and other wildlife. Clear-cutting five to ten acre blocks over a 30-year schedule gives wild-life the variously aged stands they need for food and cover at different times of the year. At the same time, the small clear-cuts will provide you with fuel and an income from the sale of logs. Properly managed, your woodlot will produce wood fiber indefinitely at a uni-form rate.

Equipment

Remember the old saw about how "wood warms you twice, once when you cut it and once when you burn it?" The right equipment will permit you to be warmed more by the burning than by the cutting.

If you are going to cut only a few trees a year, your basic equipment should be a Swedish bow saw, a split-ting maul, wedges and a sawbuck you can make your-self.

Forget that little power saw you received for Father's Day, or save it for trimming your lilac bushes. These saws are dangerous and they don't hold up under moderate use.

The next step up, where you are cutting 5 to 20 cords per year from whatever source, rent a heavy-duty pow-er saw for a few days at a time and let the rental agency worry about maintenance and sharpening. But be really concerned about safety. No amount of wood is worth a leg or an arm!

Drying and Storage

Some woods contain 100 percent or more moisture (percent of dry weight) when cut. We aim to get this down to 20 percent before burning. The first step is to let the tree lie where it falls, without being cut up. Until the leaves dry up in a few weeks, the tree will continue to lose moisture through them.

The tree can then be cut and stacked in regular cord style. For faster drying, it can be penned.

Of course, wood will dry faster if it has been cut to its usable length and split before drying. Drying will take from six to ten months.

A woodshed is not a necessity, but it does make the wood supply more accessible when the snow and ice come. It is best to bring into the house, or on a porch, a supply of wood to minimize trips out to the wood pile during the worst weather.

Ashes

Ashes should be allowed to accumulate to within an inch or two of the grate in your fireplace or several inches deep in most stoves. Check the instructions that come with your stove. To guard against the occasional hot cinder, always store ashes in a metal bucket.

Wood ash is an excellent alkaline fertilizer and in-hibits the growth of slugs, cutworms and maggots. So, after you have checked the acidity of your garden soil, apply ashes liberally. They can be spread on top of the snow in the winter or saved in a barrel for use in the spring and summer. A circle of ash around the base of fruit trees not only fertilizes, but deters insects.

Fireplace Cookery

When the old-fashioned nineteenth century picnic, with its potato salad, sandwiches and pie, encountered the twentieth century masculine appetite for more solid (and less fattening) fare, an era of open fire cookery was born. Open cookery has increased in popularity and has been refined so that it is now a delight to millions of Americans of all ages.

Grilling or roasting was found to be a joyful experience, the only regret being that the climate of much of America forbade enjoyment of outdoor meals almost half of the year. In recent years the addition of air conditioning to many new homes has tended to move the barbecue indoors.

So, open fire cookery was put on a twelve-month basis by the birth of the indoor barbecue. By indoor, we include barbecues located in enclosed porches, lanai, or in special shelters constructed near or adjoining the home. Family rooms, kitchens, and recreation rooms in basements or elsewhere are also popular. Kitchen barbecues are now available to fit right into the countertops, with built-in ventilation. Equipment is available to turn the fireplace into a barbecue, either with charcoal or the regular log fire.

Barbecues are no substitute for the ordinary routine of kitchen operation. They represent something special, something particularly in demand when guests are to be entertained or when the family is in a holiday mood—and particularly when father feels the impulse to exercise his talents as a chef.

If we begin with the open-flame cooking device in its original outdoor setting, we are confronted with the problem of location. It must not be too far from the rear entrance of the home, or the carrying of fuel, food and utensils becomes a chore. In fact, many excellent barbecues have been built against the outer wall of a house, utilizing the house chimney stack. In other instances, a garden or lawn site at a moderate distance from the house will be favored. Such a project should include visualizing the complete setting—benches and tables for the diners, plantings of shrubs or vines to afford privacy.

A competent mason who enters into the spirit of your project is a good investment. However, many men with a knack for outdoor tasks will prefer to wield the trowel themselves.

The first problem in either case is that of a proper foundation so that the structure will not settle or sag. Many prefer to excavate below the frost line, pouring a six-inch concrete foundation. However, many excel-

Custom barbecue with metal hood encourages participation of the consumer. Photo courtesy of Goodwin

lent outdoor fireplaces are supported on the "floating slab" principle. A shallow excavation is made and a concrete slab is poured with steel reinforcing installed. Six-inch by six-inch wire road mesh will do. Depending on the size of the barbecue, the slab should be from four to six inches thick and should extend at least four inches outside the boundaries of the fireplace.

In the case of amateur installations outdoors, there is sometimes a temptation to improvise metal features. A grill will be made from parallel steel rods, cemented tightly in place. The rods soon warp or sag. Expansion loosens the masonry bond. Much better to rely on a unit manufactured for the purpose by one of the reputable manufacturers listed in the back of the book. Follow manufacturer's instructions and allow for expansion.

No single unit is likely to satisfy all the desires of the open-fire chef so plan your equipment requirements with foresight. Dutch ovens, powered or hand operated spits, adjustable fire levels, and cleanout doors are among the items to be considered.

A chimney is not always necessary. If you plan to burn only charcoal, the walls around the metal units are sufficient. However, if either wood or coal is the fuel to be used, the barbecue-fireplace should have a chimney. It is also good thinking to cap the chimney to keep out rain and snow, and possibly add a screen to arrest sparks from wood fires.

If your open-fire cooking installation is to be in a new house, you probably have consulted with the architect about many features. Two things should not be overlooked—having the whole cooking area properly vented to carry off fumes, and the need for table space adjoining the cooking area to manipulate pots, pans, and utensils. Often we have encountered cases where the cooking unit was recessed in a narrow space at table height, but with no chance for the chef to maneuver.

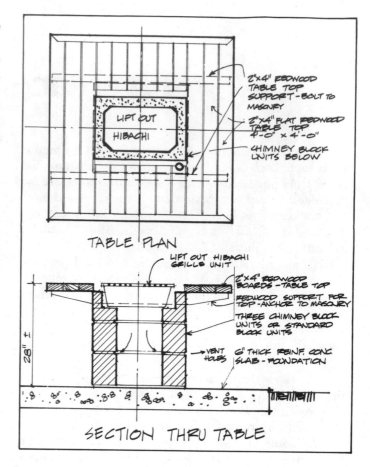

You can build this low-cost backyard barbecue yourself. Using an Hibachi charcoal grill, unit includes table, beach umbrella and concrete patio floor.

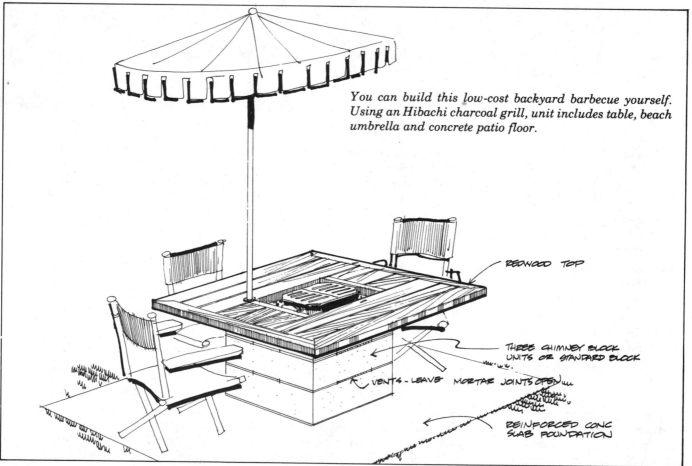

Tending an Open Fire

Some people have an instinct for fire tending; some gain fire knowledge by slow experience. Our grandfathers had fire duties from early youth, while the current crop of householders includes many who never acquired practice until a fuel shortage drove them to fire-lighting duties.

For their benefit we may say that the nineteenth century chore boy learned three stages in producing a fire, represented by the paper, the kindling wood, and the actual fuel, which might be coal or hardwood.

The match produced the flame; the paper spread it; the kindling held it, and produced enough heat to ignite the fuel with a fire that would last.

Tight homes have made the draft question so acute of late that it is a good thing to determine whether there is a decided down-draft in the chimney before starting. Wet a finger and hold it under the fireplace throat. If it is cold on the upper side, the draft is coming down. Starting a fire in that fireplace will result in a smoke filled room. Air is coming into the house through the chimney and may be consumed in combustion of the furnace or exhausted by a kitchen or bathroom ventilating fan. If opening a window a few inches or providing some other air input does not reverse the down-draft, see the following chapter to find the trouble.

In a new home, it will pay to check the effect of ventilating fans being turned on while a fire is in the hearth. If there is no way to replace this air, except down the chimney, your fireplace will smoke and ashes may be drawn onto the hearth, even through a screen.

Selecting the Fuel

Wood logs are most desirable for use in an open fireplace, though some firebuilders prefer to use coal, charcoal, or compressed sawdust logs. A wood fire is required to start other fuels.

Logs are usually available in the twenty-four-inch size. A smaller size, sixteen inches in length, is called stove wood. Larger logs to three feet and longer are available for king-sized fireplaces. Logs may be split or whole, although split logs start burning faster.

Well seasoned hardwoods such as beech, hickory, oak, maple, and most fruitwoods are preferable to softwoods such as pine and evergreens, although these make excellent kindling.

The softwoods usually burn too fast, but for this reason, they may be desirable if you want a roaring fire "right now."

Apple and hickory give a pleasant aroma. Hickory is preyed upon by carpenter bugs that may infest the premises. Elm logs that have been killed by the Dutch Elm disease are to be avoided to minimize contamination of other elms in your neighborhood. Madrone, manzanita, and eucalyptus are used in the west.

Kindling can be any species, split into little sticks less than three-fourths of an inch thick. Branches accumulated from tree pruning on your property will do the job well when dry. Pine boughs saved from your Christmas tree work well as do pinecones used in conjunction with kindling wood.

Cannel coal is one of the popular coals for fireplace use. It is the next thing to an oil-bearing shale, ignites quickly, sputters a good deal and makes a lot of ash. A fire screen is good caution when burning cannel but a screen diminishes heat and mars enjoyment.

Kentucky coals have earned a fine reputation as fireplace coal. They ignite easily, burn brightly, with a minimum of fine powder-like ash without clinkers. There are other kinds of bituminous coals that burn acceptably in open fires.

Of course, charcoal is favored for cooking in the fireplace and some fire tenders prefer it or charcoal mixed with wood for their regular fires. Charcoal radiates about twice as much heat as wood and charcoal briquets are even better. Odorless, invisible carbon monoxide is given off by charcoal, so adequate ventilation should always be provided.

Ocean driftwood will burn with a blue and lavender fire. Other colorful fires can be produced by soaking firewood, pinecones, or charcoal in various salt solutions. Use strontium chloride or nitrate for a red flame. Common table salt (sodium chloride) makes a yellow fire. Green and blue flames are produced by copper chloride.

Avoid the use of scrap lumber (except for kindling), refuse or Christmas wrappings as they may produce a great many sparks which could become a fire hazard.

Laying the Fire

Much of the literature of New England must have been produced in front of log fires, if we draw inference from continual allusions to the fire and to fire lighting. There was (and is) a positive ritual of back logs and fore logs, of preference in wood.

Let us see if we can reduce these dogmas to general principles. We have seen that a fire must (1) be lit, (2) be spread, and (3) be held until general ignition takes place. The final stage of fire tending is to conserve it and keep the fuel from burning up too rapidly.

Andirons are usually placed twelve to sixteen inches apart, centered on the hearth. If you build a fire daily, leave some of yesterday's ashes, brushed together as a foundation for today's bed of coals. Place three or four inches of twisted or crumpled newspaper on the hearth between the andirons. Arrange kindling criss-cross on the papers. If a firebasket is used, the kindling fire may be placed in or under the basket, allowing air space.

Set up two four- to five-inch logs across the andirons with the thickest, longest, or greenest about one-half of an inch away from the back. Leave a few inches between the back log and the front log (preferably split). Place a split log on top, arranged so it leaves room for the flames to come through.

Function of a Back Log If your wood supply contains some pieces that are hard to burn, perhaps green, do not be disappointed. They make fine back logs. The back log lies against the back of the fireplace. You lean split pine or faggots against it in kindling your fire. It makes a counter surface for livelier-burning wood and helps to hold the body of the blaze forward where it will do the most good.

Wood that is fairly green can be burned after the fire is well under way, especially if there is a good bed of coals. It should be split finer than is necessary with dry, seasoned wood.

English Fire-Laying Method Here is a method of laying a wood fire much used in England. Newspapers are first crumpled between the andirons, then two logs are laid parallel with a space between, over the paper. Kindling is laid across these logs, spread about an inch apart, with a few sticks standing vertically down into the paper. Then the third log is placed on top, parallel with the bottom logs. This arrangement creates a quick flame with good draft between the logs.

It is said that the English have developed this system because wood is very scarce and it is considered essential to have a nice, newly laid fire blazing in the hall or guest room immediately when a visitor arrives—as essential as their little courtesy of polishing shoes overnight.

Teepee Fire-Laying Method A teepee formation of kindling and small branch wood will ease your fire through early combustion stages until the logs are aglow. Place these logs close. The narrow air spaces between them promote better drafts. The heat reflected between adjacent surfaces aids in raising and maintaining combustion temperatures.

The most common error of neophytes with a fireplace is to try to burn one log of wood at a time. Even two logs are apt to snuff out. Three units in your wood fireplace represent a practical minimum.

Good fire-builders recognize that the growing flame needs the protection of fuel around it—that it thrives best when twisting upward between fagots or chunks that continually obstruct it, continually force it to twist and turn.

Before lighting the kindling, lay about one sheet of crumpled newspaper on the logs. Lighting this moments before lighting the kindling warms the flue and establishes a draft.

Contrary to general belief a fire of coal or wood can be held overnight in a fireplace. First, leave a bed of coals with some unburned fuel on top, cover the fireplace opening with a piece of sheet metal, except for three or four inches at the top. A little practice will bring gratifying results in conditions where this overnight fire is desirable.

Building a Coal Fire Coal is a more stable fuel than wood and requires less attention, but it does not have the cheerful blaze of wood, although it is kindled in much the same manner. If you have a good "grate" coal, the blaze will be well established in fifteen minutes, but be careful not to crowd too much in. The flue should be warmed gradually and each piece of coal placed carefully until a lively coal flame has been achieved.

Igniting Devices To many city dwellers, the problem of kindling wood is quite as acute as that of getting firewood. To them a mechanical lighting device makes sense.

A built-in gas fired log starter is often used for this

purpose. An electric fire starter is also available. A Cap Cod lighter is a device with a metal handle and a head of absorbent fireclay which rests in a small kettle of kerosene. Removed and lighted it acts as a wick and ignites the coal or wood used as a fuel. However, the absorbent fireclay becomes heated and if the fire does not soon ignite, do not re-immerse the lighter in the oil immediately or oil may explode.

Pouring gasoline or oil on the fire to get it started? Don't! Even charcoal lighter fluid should be used with care.

Use of Fire Tools It is a sign of bad fire tending to lift a coal hod and throw a large part of its contents on the flame. Better to place each chunk where needed with the tongs, or to lift out moderate-sized shovelfuls with the fire shovel.

The poker should be used to rouse the flame by opening new draft passages among the embers and by rearranging the fuel. In the case of wood fires, there is repeated need to bring the unburned ends of logs into the center of the fire, and a poker, or tongs, makes easy work of this task. A brush is useful in cleaning the hearth or keeping the ashes in a neat pile. Some people like to use a bellows as a persuader for a lagging flame.

Make sure that the damper is wide open before you light your fire. Many fireplaces are operated with dampers constantly open. Dampers do not have to be constantly opened and closed in order to be of great value in promoting smooth discharge of smoke and arresting down-draft.

When the fire-builder has mastered other features of fireplace operation, he can begin experimenting to see how much his damper opening can be cut down, with his fuel, and save heat while discharging all the smoke. When only a bed of glowing coal remains, the damper can be brought nearest to a closed position. But be sure to open it before refueling with smoke-producing fuel.

Use a pair of fire tongs to stand any unburned logs on end in the back corners of the fireplace. They will soon go out and you will have some good kindling ready for the next fire. When retiring for the night, leave the damper open and the screen closed, to be sure that no chance ignition will cause trouble while you sleep.

Fireplace Difficulties

Properly constructed fireplaces burn warmly, cleanly, safely. Those owners who "guess all fireplaces smoke" are making the wrong guess. Yet faulty construction is common enough. Investigation nearly always reveals some basic fault in planning, or some mistake of execution or operation.

Smokiness

The great majority of complaints about fireplace operation are based on smoky operation. Here are some of the conditions and remedies that relate to smokiness.

Fireplace Too Large for Flue The flue area should not be less than the area of the fireplace opening. Where too small to carry off products of combustion, remedy may be found in reducing the size of the opening. Some corrective workers (1) install a shallow hood of metal beneath the fireplace breast. This also helps in cases where the damper position is too low. (2) Other ways of reducing the opening are to raise the hearth by laying one or two courses of brick over the old hearth. (3) Where drastic reduction is needed narrow the sides of the opening.

Damper Too Low Smokiness often ensues because the damper has been installed with its front flange at the lower level of the front wall, serving as a support for the brickwork. The remedy is to lower the top of the opening by adding one or two courses of brick, resting on an angle lintel.

Lack of Combustion Air Recent innovations in caulking and weatherstripping have made homes so tight that there are no air inlets to provide air for oxygen and for draft, such as every fire needs. The result is that the unlighted fireplace becomes an inlet for outdoor air. If the furnace, the cooking range and incinerator are lighted, there is a steady current of air down the fireplace chimney.

Then if the fireplace is lighted, the draft down the chimney is pretty sure to drive smoke out into the room. We have repeatedly investigated complaints of smoky fireplaces which proved to be due to lack of ventilation for the interior as a whole. Often opening a basement window an inch or two would cause the fire to burn brightly. The only answer to this type of fireplace trouble is ventilation—not merely for the fireplace, but for the furnace, incinerator, range, etc. It is a poor sort of progress that excludes air from interiors where people are supposed to live.

Leakage from Flue to Flue Sometimes smoke will issue from a fireplace that has no fire in it. Search will show that flues have been placed side by side in the same stack without cementing the joints between units of flue lining. If a furnace fire is burning briskly, there is apt to be down-draft in the fireplace flue, for reasons stated. Smoke will be sucked across through the uncemented flue lining joints and descend (providing principles outlined above are disregarded)—coming out of the fireplace. The remedy is to close such passages. Staggering units of the lining is a help.

Use of Perforated Brick Where workmanship is good, there can be no objection to the use of perforated brick in chimney work. Where a job is carelessly done, the fact that brick is perforated may account for the emission of smoke at a point that cannot otherwise be accounted for. The fault, in such cases, is with the workmanship, not the material.

Leakage Impairs Draft Where flue joints are uncemented and mortar in surrounding brickwork disintegrates, there is often a leakage of air into the chimney. This prevents the chimney from exercising the draft possibilities which its height would otherwise assure. The case is similar to that of trying to smoke a cigarette with a hole in the paper. Thorough pointing of the brickwork usually effects a cure.

Wind Deflected Down Chimney The surroundings of a home may have a marked bearing on fireplace performance. If located at the foot of a bluff or hill, or if there are high trees close at hand, the result may be to deflect wind down the chimney in heavy gusts. A nearby high building has been known to produce the same effect. Installing a hooded chimney is a common and efficient way of dealing with this difficulty. It may also be mentioned that carrying the flue lining a few inches above the brickwork, with a bevel of cement around it, is a recognized means of promoting clean exit of smoke from the flue. It minimizes wind eddies. The cement bevel also causes moisture to drain from the top and prevents frost troubles between linings and masonry.

"Pouring" from Flue to Flue We have spoken of the case where down-draft from interior suction pulls smoke from the top of one flue down an adjoining flue. Related to this is the case where vertical wind currents force smoke down an inactive flue as it emerges from an adjoining flue. One way to treat this is to carry the flues to different heights above the masonry. In other cases, multiple flues are capped. Note the bevel of cement which helps drainage and promotes clean emission of smoke.

Cases of Flue Leakage There are various cases

where smoke or odors will pervade a home through faulty chimney construction. One type of difficulty comes from the butting of open tile against a flue. Unless the joint of the flue is tight and remains so, it will emit smoke through the hollow tile, and may issue at a point remote from the fireplace and prompt a call for the fire department.

Proper Joint Practice   The safeguards against conditions cited are threefold—(1) Careful cementing of flue joints, space between flue lining and brickwork being filled with mortar, (2) Staggering of joints in adjoining flues, or at least four inches of well-cemented brick between flues, (3) Surrounding brickwork properly laid and joined.

Method of Sealing Joints   A method of closing uncemented flue joints without tearing out the chimney has been used with success in some instances. It involves the use of a traveling plug and fairly thin grout. As a plug, a canvas bag is sometimes employed, stuffed with rags or papers and weighted with bricks in the bottom. When lowered into a flue from the top, by means of a line or pole, it should fit fairly tight, but not too tight for motion. The method of use is to stop it just below the level of each flue joint and pour grout down the flue. When stopped by the plug, the grout flows into the open joint. After the joint appears filled, the plug may be lifted and lowered a few times, producing a swabbing effect. Then it is lowered to the succeeding joint and the operation repeated.

This operation should be carried out with a careful eye to conditions in the fireplace below. If too much grout is passing the plug, it may pile up on the smoke shelf, drain into the fireplace and deface it, or, in hardening, may impair the working of the damper.

Flue Off Center   The flue should always take off from the center of the smoke chamber and, if a slope is necessary, it should occur above that point. When the flue takes off from one side, it produces uneven draft. Smoke travels sluggishly from the farther side of the fire area and is prone to eddy out into the room. Correction calls for rebuilding the smoke chamber and realigning of the flue.

Double Use of Fireplace Flue   Where kitchen stove, furnace or other appliance uses the same flue as the fireplace, there is always a danger of smoking and draft disturbances. Each fireplace should have its own flue.

Flue Choked by Debris   The commonest form which this difficulty takes is the deposit of mortar, carelessly dropped down the chimney during construction. If the flue is straight, debris generally lodges on the smoke shelf and may impede the working of the damper. This condition may be corrected by disconnecting the control device, lifting out the valve plate and removing the debris through the fireplace throat. In case there are turns in the flue, debris may lodge at the angle and such debris is sometimes found to include broken pieces of brick and flue tile. In some instances such obstructions can be dislodged from above by a pole or weighted line and debris removed from the smoke shelf. More often it involves tearing out.

Choking at Base of Flue   The upper course of brick in the smoke chamber should offset just enough to afford support for the flue lining, without impinging on the area of the opening. Frequently it is found that bricks have been set in such a way as to reduce the area of the flue. The only remedy involves removing the obstruction. The same effect might be produced by a cap that chokes the outlet.

Sooty Fireplace Face   Should the face of your fireplace become stained with smoke and soot, clean it with a mild acid bleach, such as vinegar or acetic acid, or scour with strong soap and water. Stubborn stains can be scrubbed with a solution of hydrochloric (muriatic) acid. Rubber gloves, please! Do not use on stonework. It may also discolor some types of brick. Mixture is one part acid to ten parts water. Rinse off with water immediately. This treatment will also remove construction stains from mortar, etc.

Of course, if you avoid getting the fireplace dirty, you don't have to clean it. Avoid burning trash and paper in large amounts as your flue is not sized for this sudden load.

Flue Lining Out of Line   Sometimes careless masons fail to set flue lining with due alignment, leaving uneven joints, prone to cause leakage of smoke and fumes. In some instances where a slight change of direction in the flue is necessary, it is done—not by sloping the flue in the proper manner—but by successive offsets of vertical lining.

One Fireplace Below Another   Two fairly common mistakes in building a recreation room fireplace below a living room fireplace are—(1) Using one flue for both. (2) Taking off the flue for the lower fireplace at the side of the smoke chamber, in order to carry it around the fireplace above. The lower fireplace should be offset sufficiently so that a flue from the lower fireplace bypasses the upper one and reaches the chimney stack by a slope of not more than 7 inches to the foot.

Ashpit Clogged   Difficulty sometimes encountered in removing ashes from ashpits points to the need of making pits with uniform sectional areas and smooth walls. When pits or chutes are offset in passing a fireplace on a lower floor, all possible care must be taken to avoid roughness or sharp changes of direction. Wall leakage, particularly in the basement wall, permits water to seep in and convert ashes into a soaked and tightly packed mass. The ashpit door should be centered at the base of the pit and be large enough to afford access, by poker, to free clogged masses near the base. More difficult conditions may call for tearing out masonry and treating obstructions.

Moisture and Frost Troubles Because chimneys are subject to contrast of inner and outer temperatures, there is more tendency for mortar to crack and disintegrate than in wall masonry. Natural gas fumes, which form a vapor, may escape through uncemented flue joints and augment the effect of moisture. Cottages left vacant during the winter are particularly subject to moisture and frost troubles.

Moisture in masonry is always a menace, because it freezes in cold weather and causes disintegration of mortar and spalling of the brickwork. The greatest source of danger is the chimney top. There should be a smooth, impervious bevel of cement at the top, closing the joint between brickwork and lining. If this bevel cracks, and admits moisture between lining and brickwork, disintegration is rapid. The chimney becomes a menace because high winds may blow it down. Joint leakage is a lesser evil. Capping the flue is a safeguard against moisture entering the inside of the flue.

Chimneys should be kept under observation for the need of pointing, and their tops examined periodically. Mastic pointing is more effective than cement pointing because mastic adheres better and repels water. Roof cement makes an excellent pointing material.

Use of Fire Basket Where a fire is built directly on the hearth, it has somewhat the effect of increasing the size of the fireplace opening, and a larger flue may be desirable. Conversely, installing a fire basket may cure trouble from an inadequate flue.

Where the breast of the fireplace is thick, trouble may result from placing the basket too far forward. In general it is safest to have the front of the basket no farther forward than the rear line of the breast. A little experimenting in basket position will show where it yields the most heat with minimum risk of smoke eddies.

Troubles Generally Avoidable With comparatively rare exceptions, the troubles that owners suffer from their fireplaces are easily avoidable. It costs little, if anything, more to build a fireplace correctly than to build it badly. Against the varied array of difficulties we have mentioned must be counted the millions of fireplaces that operate to produce uniform warmth, cheer and contentment. Corrective work may involve considerable tearing out, but is preferable to long endurance of an unsatisfactory fireplace.

Index

Metric Conversion Tables

Length Conversions

fractional inch	millimeters	fractional inch	millimeters
1/32	.7938	17/32	13.49
1/16	1.588	9/16	14.29
3/32	2.381	19/32	15.08
1/8	3.175	5/8	15.88
5/32	3.969	21/32	16.67
3/16	4.763	11/16	17.46
7/32	5.556	23/32	18.26
1/4	6.350	3/4	19.05
9/32	7.144	25/32	19.84
5/16	7.938	13/16	20.64
11/32	8.731	27/32	21.43
3/8	9.525	7/8	22.23
13/32	10.32	29/32	23.02
7/16	11.11	15/16	23.81
15/32	11.91	31/32	24.61
1/2	12.70	1	25.40

feet	meters	feet	meters
1	.3048	8	2.438
1½	.4572	8½	2.591
2	.6096	9	2.743
2½	.7620	9½	2.896
3	.9144	10	3.048
3½	1.067	10½	3.200
4	1.219	11	3.353
4½	1.372	11½	3.505
5	1.524	12	3.658
5½	1.676	15	4.572
6	1.829	20	6.096
6½	1.981	25	7.620
7	2.133	50	15.24
7½	2.286	100	30.48

inches	centimeters	inches	centimeters
1	2.54	5	12.70
1¼	3.175	5¼	13.34
1½	3.81	5½	13.97
1¾	4.445	5¾	14.61
2	5.08	6	15.24
2¼	5.715	6½	16.51
2½	6.35	7	17.78
2¾	6.985	7½	19.05
3	7.62	8	20.32
3¼	8.255	8½	21.59
3½	8.89	9	22.86
3¾	9.525	9½	24.13
4	10.16	10	25.40
4¼	10.80	10½	26.67
4½	11.43	11	27.94
4¾	12.07	11½	29.21

Common Conversion Factors

	Given the number of	To obtain the number of	Multiply by
Length	inches	centimeters (cm)	2.54
	feet	decimeters (dm)	3.05
	yards	meters (m)	0.91
	miles	kilometers (km)	1.61
	millimeters (mm)	inches	0.039
	centimeters	inches	0.39
	meters	yards	1.09
	kilometers	miles	0.62
Area	square inches	square centimeters (cm²)	6.45
	square feet	square meters (m²)	0.093
	square yards	square meters	0.84
	square miles	square kilometers (km²)	2.59
	acres	hectares (ha)	0.40
	square centimeters	square inches	0.16
	square meters	square yards	1.20
	square kilometers	square miles	0.39
	hectares	acres	2.47
Mass or weight	grains	milligrams (mg)	64.8
	ounces	grams (g)	28.3
	pounds	kilograms (kg)	0.45
	short tons	megagrams (metric tons)	0.91
	milligrams	grains	0.015
	grams	ounces	0.035
	kilograms	pounds	2.21
	megagrams	short tons	1.10
Capacity or volume	fluid ounces	milliliter (ml)	29.8
	pints (fluid)	liters (l)	0.47
	quarts (fluid)	liters	0.95
	gallons (fluid)	liters	3.80
	cubic inches	cubic centimeters (cm³)	16.4
	cubic feet	cubic meters (m³)	0.028
	cubic feet	liters	28.3
	bushels (dry)	liters	35.2
	milliliters	ounces	0.034
	liters	pints	2.11
	liters	quarts	1.06
	liters	gallons	0.26
	liters	cubic feet	0.035
	cubic centimeters	cubic inches	0.061
	cubic meters	cubic feet	35.3
	cubic meters	bushels	28.4
Temperature	degrees Fahrenheit	degrees Celsius	0.556 (after subtracting 32)
	degrees Celsius	degrees Fahrenheit	1.80 (then add 32)